GARDENING WITH STYLE

A PRIVATE VIEW OF THE WORLD'S MOST INNOVATIVE GARDENS

GARDENING WITH STYLE

A PRIVATE VIEW OF THE WORLD'S MOST INNOVATIVE GARDENS

PETER KING · CAROLE OTTESEN · GRAHAM ROSE

DIAGRAMS BY WILF CHAMBERS

BLOOMSBURY

First published in Great Britain 1988
Copyright © 1988 by Peter King, Carole Ottesen &
Graham Rose

Bloomsbury Publishing Ltd, 2 Soho Square,
London W1V 5DE

British Library Cataloguing in Publication Data
  Rose, Graham
  Gardening with style: a private view of the world's most
  innovative gardens
  1. Gardening
  I. Title   II. King, Peter   III. Ottesen, Carole
  635   SB450.97
  ISBN 0-7475-0080-0

Designed by Laurence Bradbury and Roy Williams
Assisted by Sarah Collins and Colin Woodman

Front cover shows York Gate, Adel, near Leeds, the garden
of the Spencers; back cover shows a garden in the Woolhara
suburb of Sydney, Australia, designed by Trevor Crump;
title page shows Gilles Clement's garden; previous page,
one of the flower borders at Biggar Park.

Printed in Italy by Imago Publishing Ltd

Contents

INTRODUCTION

'When are we going to see the garden?' the late Duke of Westminster asked his wife as they walked together around the grounds of a famous plantsman's house. She pointed out that they had been walking round it for over half an hour. The Duke was amazed. Where was the lawn, the flowerbeds, the path down the middle, and the fence at the end? No garden was a garden unless it had its lawn and herbaceous borders, believed the Duke, and many of us feel the same.

This book is about people who *don't* feel that a garden is a garden is a garden. They take the opposite view, that the greatest pleasure comes from the creative process, rather than from gardening for its own sake. They wish to apply their own sense of style to their gardens, and believe that a garden – like a room or a house – can be an extension of the personality. This does not mean that the gardens chosen for this book are a radical departure from those all around us – although some are: the American, A. E. Bye, whose gardens 'look as if nothing at all has been done,' would certainly have amazed the Duke of Westminster.

Nor are all the gardeners in this book professionals. Some are, and some came to gardening from allied disciplines like painting, architecture, or interior design. The criterion for choosing them has simply been that each has applied a strong individual style of his or her own. Their choice does not imply that the authors believe these are the only stylish gardeners to be found or the only ones worth writing about. It is certainly acknowledged that other influential gardeners such as Geoffrey Jellicoe and Keith Steadman might well have been included. The latter once made the pertinent remark that after 30 years of only thinking of gardens, he suddenly realised that 'it is fun to grow things because they make nice shapes.' As a painter, he had views on what made a nice shape. This book is about 40 such gardeners, perhaps less widely publicised than Steadman, who have similarly stopped thinking of gardens as gardens 'ought to look'.

We have mostly chosen men and women whose style can be seen in the totality of their gardens. They have imprinted themselves across the whole canvas. The point is worth making because almost everyone who gardens has at least small touches of individual style. For example, there is a block of flats near the Tate Gallery in London with a few shrubs in containers in a very gloomy area below tenement-type buildings; what makes the display stylish are the extraordinary colours which the tin containers have been painted. An example at the other extreme: two French sculptors have decorated a garden by hanging bronze apples in an orchard, but their apples have

Small touches of individual style, such as pleasing buildings, can sometimes be extended to the whole, as when John Last decided to ennoble almost the entire garden of a small terraced house with this garage of unusual character.

8

A topiary garden is an idiom derived from another century, but it can be of our own day, like Beckley Park

smiling faces reminiscent of the golden apples of the Hesperides. In the cabbage patch is another cabbage-sized bronze head which qualifies for admission because it has cabbage-leaf hair. The owners have added many more such touches here and there to make a stylish point, or sometimes a stylish joke.

What, then, is style in gardening? One of the most famous of twentieth-century gardeners, Russell Page, described it like this nearly thirty years ago:

Where does style start? Style for the garden designer means to assemble all the physical elements of a garden scene, to blend them into a coherent whole, and to imbue this whole with all the intensity or, perhaps I should say 'intelligence', that he can muster, so that the whole may have a quality peculiar to itself. Such style must be con-

temporary, since, if a composition has style, it must reflect its maker's intention, and its maker is necessarily of his own day, even though he may have chosen to give his garden an idiom derived from another place or another century. Here I would like to differentiate between style and decoration. I could consider no modern garden even remotely interesting as a work of art unless it could stand as such, stripped of every single purely decorative attribute. A garden artist will only use decoration to heighten the style, that is, the idea from which his whole construction has sprung.

'The idea from which his whole construction has sprung' does not take us very far because it is only another way of talking about style. In general it seems far easier to say what style is not. Sir Roy Strong, the art and garden historian, tells us that 'it is not about money, nor is it confined to any social strata.' More positively, he says that 'it is really an attitude. An ability to make mundane things seem extraordinary, or the extraordinary look even more extraordinary. Or sometimes the talent to make extraordinary things seem very ordinary. People whose work possesses style have the ability to do everything against the rules and produce marvellous results.'

'The rules of design and taste can be learnt,' Sir Roy continues, warming to the theme. 'You can learn about colour harmonies and their control, the massing and grouping of plants, the laws of perspective. What you can't learn is the flair to break the rules successfully. This means that a work could be judged perfect and remain style-less. Perhaps because it wasn't an extension of the personality of its creator, it didn't express an identifiable personal vision.'

And then, reverting to the negatives in a very positive manner, he proclaims 'Style is never vulgar ostentation.'

Lord Snowdon, son of one of our most stylish gardeners, Lady Rosse, also uses negatives in his definition: 'It is something you can't buy,' though it is often 'copied by the unimaginative and un-talented through the pages of the glossies . . . It is neither to do with prettiness nor glamour – it's neither obvious nor overstated – it's an expression of that particular person – an indescribable, unique quality – a mixture of inventive chic and personal quality of design – the opposite to "kitsch".'

Piet Oudolf, the Dutch landscape architect, feels that designers with style can strongly influence the way that other designers approach their tasks. And, sadly, these days he finds that he is very short of inspiration. 'Most landscaping these days consists of trends and copies. What I call the little Sissinghurst and little Versailles mentality; as a landscape architect, I don't find it renewing. The simple formula of making more

levels and enlarging the pond might satisfy clients but it is hardly likely to result in style. My approach is that the architectural elements should be so strong that even when the green elements develop, they will still be clearly recognisable. I also tend to use many plants which themselves have a strong architectural quality.'

There has long been a certain internationalism about gardening, with travellers bringing back home ideas as well as new plants. Today,

There is nothing un-stylish about hanging a bird box on a tree trunk, but curious sculptures from another culture, as well as being more original, may give a garden an accent of its own

9

'Use imagination and make it original' is highly appropriate to Ian Hamilton-Finlay who here hangs one of his visual conundrums in a tree

10

the process is faster, with jet travel, videos and TV and the widespread use of colour in all the media. One result of this may be that the famous gardens of the past are now so well publicised as to make it inevitable that the powerful personalities of the past come to dominate contemporary designs. One writer on gardening, Mary Keen, asserts that 'the historical approach dominates private gardening today . . . Reproductions of knot gardens and *parterres* abound and even non-gardeners have heard of Sissinghurst.' While another writer and designer, John Brookes, agrees with her ('It cannot be healthy to advance into retrospect . . . we have latched on to Miss Jekyll as our last original garden thinker.'), he seems to believe, as we do, that 'increasingly a new light shines' and 'there is a mood upon the wind.' He admits that 'as yet it has not manifested itself in any particular design form.' We believe this is just as well: gardening has suffered for too long from a slavish following of the current style in fashion. To make a break with the past it is necessary to follow the advice of that famous gardener Sir John Thouron: 'Use imagination and make it original.'

If it is true that the adoption of historical models is far too widespread, then it is also true that men and women can be found all over the world who are kicking over the traces. Some are featured in this book. Our examples come from a wide range of countries and climates. Some have developed ideas which have spread far beyond their country of origin while others are scarcely known outside a small circle of admirers. All of them have in common the desire to imprint a personality on their own garden. This personality or style is readily apparent. One of Sir Roy Strong's *bon mots* is that 'style is the sixth millionth Chinese wearing his Mao jacket while marching along with the other five million, nine hundred thousand, nine hundred and ninety nine. But he is wearing his jacket the wrong way round and looks marvellous.' Style, like the Chinaman, is readily recognised.

Quality, not quantity, has been our criterion in choosing gardeners. If it has been their quantitative influence, then we should certainly have included Burle Marx of Brazil. He needs a book to himself, but it is right to comment on his influence here because it has been so profound.

Burle Marx brought exotic plants from the Brazilian jungle to a 'civilised' setting. Here is part of his large nursery of what were, until 1950, virtually unknown species

11

Painting in plants, magnificent tile murals and pavements like this one are the elements of Burle Marx's contribution to the changing face of Brazil

12

exuberance of nature – 'her huge tropical leaves, the coiling tendrils of plants, the meandering course of the Amazon.'

It has been said that 'it is quite easy to super-impose many of his garden designs over his paintings.' In broad terms his gardening is decoration in two dimensions. The soil is his canvas. He applies plants, mosaics, stone and grass as an artist might apply paint. There is a horizontality about his work which marks him out from the essentially three-dimensional grandeur of the classic European gardeners – although this is not to say that his work lacks sculptural effect. But, essentially, 'painting with plants' requires a flat, low ground-cover treatment which in the tropics is achieved by mass planting of temporary bedding plants, such as *coleus* and *alternanthera*, which are frequently renewed. 'Gardening is just the same as painting and the plastic arts,' says Burle Marx. 'Gardens are works in contrasts and harmonies; simply speaking, the enactment of clear thinking, no matter if it were painting, drawing or gardens.'

While still in his twenties, Marx the painter met and worked with some of the most advanced architects of his time, including the Swiss Le Corbusier. His work included a tile mural and gardens filled with native Brazilian flora, rarely used in cultivated gardens at that time. These two strands in his development – the architectural and the use of tropical plants – have come to have an immense influence outside Brazil. Sir Peter Shepherd the architect recalls that 'his influence was first seen in Europe at the Festival of Britain – both on the South Bank and in Battersea Park. He changed all our visions by making a positive connection between landscaping and architecture.'

Those who are unfamiliar with Marx's work directly (and the majority of it is in Brazil) will recall that over the past twenty years there has been a growing tendency in America and Europe

The key to Marx's development as a gardener lies in his painting. He was trained as a painter and remains a painter, despite his full-time activities as a professional landscape gardener, and has exhibited in nine countries on more than thirty occasions. Marx's style as a painter gives a clue to his style as a landscape gardener. His work is largely abstract, using segmented areas blocked in with colour, influenced, he has said, by European abstract and cubist painting. But a more likely influence, it has been suggested, is the

to fill office blocks with green jungles of figs, yuccas, bamboos and papyrus. Is this, they may wonder, the influence of Burle Marx? Often it is, and it is doubtful whether the passion for the atrium in department stores, hotel foyers and offices would have developed so extensively had it not been for his disciples spreading what they took to be the gospel of the master.

Burle Marx himself developed his art out of the inspiration of the Brazilian *mata* – great, vast, untouched areas, almost surreal in their profusion. Can his inspiration have been wholly contained in modest entrance halls to office blocks in Liverpool or Akron, Ohio? Again, Marx has not taken vast numbers of species and dumped them together in a heterogeneous jungle. His art is to segregate and isolate species to bring out their individual character. In contrast, his disciples sometimes appear to believe that it is their role to re-create the jungle in a 'civilised' setting. Of course, Marx does design in order to juxtapose varieties, sometimes making quite extraordinary contrasts, but the skill with which he does so is 'painterly' and very stylish.

To 'do your own thing' may of course lead to an eccentricity which some would regard as un-stylish. The late Stephen Spender was talking about clothes rather than gardening when he said style was made up of 'three parts natural grace, one part sense of period, and two parts eccentricity.' There is no reason why a little eccentricity should not be part of the recipe for success and some of the gardeners in this book certainly have it. So do many gardeners who, for one reason or another, are not included in these pages. One of these was the late Edith, Marchioness of Londonderry, who planted a garden in Mount Stewart in Ulster to recall a famous ancestor of legend. She has a stone shamrock across which is sprawled the Bloody Hand of Ulster, a composition of red dwarf begonias. Behind this, in topiary, is a strange Irish harp of

Instead of building a pool for his waterlilies, a stylish gardener might pick up this hint from Thailand and grow his lilies in individual dragon pots

13

the type seen on a bottle of Guinness. Topiary work is where style and eccentricity probably come closer together than anywhere else in the garden. This also illustrates Lord Snowdon's point that style is not a matter of money: topiary is basically the result of patience and imagination.

It is true that some of the gardeners in this book have spent a great deal of money in the course of evolving their style. In part they may have done so to speed the process by buying mature trees and shrubs rather than waiting for cuttings or small plants to grow. Others have spent considerable sums on wooden furniture ('Curves are very expensive,' warns David Hicks.) It is nevertheless not necessary to spend large sums of money in order to bring imagination and character into a garden, although perhaps it sometimes helps. John Brookes be-

14

Breaking away from the Victorian bird nets comes easily to Ian Hamilton-Finlay who, with a marine theme to his whole garden, chooses to cover his strawberry pots with coloured fish nets over a sail-like structure

lieves that the increased wealth of the 'haves' in contrast to the 'have nots' has played a significant part in the changes in garden design in recent years. He cites an increased use of machinery. The thesis of this book is that, rather than responding to their environment, stylish gardeners are original thinkers who *manage* its change.

Our purpose is to encourage gardeners to be original in their approach. Unless this happens on a broader scale, gardening will atrophy or, if that is too strong a word, we shall go on designing in aspic. Mary Keen bemoans 'the state of garden design in England today' and perhaps her criticism might be applied to other countries too.

Fortunately there are gardeners who are breaking away from the Victorian/Jekyll/Robinson concept with its over-dominant lawn and herbaceous border. The gardeners featured here show, in their different ways, how that break may be made. If we have not, in the process, precisely defined that elusive word 'style' then we beg to be excused and can only point to our gardeners.

One last point. When we began this book it was the intention to describe the work of living gardeners. While it was in the course of publication two of those written about have died, Pietro Porcinai and Robert Heber-Percy, and we dedicate the book to their memory.

An atmosphere of a world apart – somewhere not quite tamed – has been created by Gilles Clement in his own garden

THE NEW FORMALISTS

Globes of tightly clipped yew and box fronting an Italianate loggia provide the herb garden at York Gate with a pleasing formality while repeating the spherical theme used to produce topiary or stone finials elsewhere in the garden

GEORGE CLIVE

TINKERING WITH THE LANDSCAPE

George Clive produced a charming eighteenth-century vista using twentieth-century machines at surprisingly low cost

Gardening with style demands a certain confidence and panache; an ability to dream up ambitious projects and ensure their execution with unflinching determination. These are the attributes with which George Clive is richly endowed and he has used them on his

land near Hereford to good effect. There, in lovely rolling countryside, he has created one of the largest scale private gardens made in Britain during the last half of the twentieth century. Setting him apart from most serious farmers and foresters, gardening for George Clive has become a major free-time obsession. It is astonishing that the work he has done himself and the relatively small investment which he has made have had such a significant impact on the landscape.

He was fortunate that, by thoughtful planting of mixed evergreen and deciduous trees, his ancestors created an attractive parkland frame around the view from the south façade of his house. However, the nearground consisted of a rather uninteresting gravelled terrace. And since this area lay directly outside the main living rooms, when George Clive became responsible for the land, it was this part of the garden which he improved first. Paving the terrace with formal stone slabs, he built four stone-walled raised beds and divided the terrace by planting transverse hedges. The beds were crowned with spectacular mounds of the rose Blanc Double de Coubert – dominating lilies like *Lilium regale* and *Lilium henryi*.

Clive stationed a splendid figure of Ceres as a high point at one end of the terrace. On a rectangular lawn south of the terrace he made his first gesture towards the grand gardening which

subsequently became his passion. On the premises of a firm near London which specialises in antique garden ornaments he discovered a large eighteenth-century octagonal basin which was in very poor condition and was consequently sold at auction for a reasonable price. Transporting it in pieces half-way across England, he re-erected it as a centrepiece on the lawn and carefully restored it to something approaching its former grandeur. To add colour to the lawn area, Clive made beds to back it which were devoted to herbaceous plants with a heavy emphasis on lilies such as *L. speciosum*, *L. martagon* (*album* and *dalmaticum*) and *L. henryi*.

To the east there was another large lawn dominated by an ancient cedar. George Clive now manages this as a wildflower meadow – cutting it for hay in early August and topping it again to tidy it in October. This has become an attractive haven for orchids, including frog, green-winged, common spotted, heath spotted and a host of twablades.

Once Clive had satisfied himself that the south garden was complete he turned his attention to the other side of the house where, across the driveway from the main entrance and down some steps, there was an overgrown goldfish pond which had been made in the nineteenth century.

In the course of improving the driveway wall and the flight of steps down to the water's edge,

GEORGE CLIVE: Whitfield

A House
B Conservatory 1781
C Kitchen garden
D Stables
E Swimming pool
F Goldfish pond
G Tennis courts
H Canal
I Castle pond
J Lime avenue
K Park

1 Terrace
2 Lawn
3 Fountain and basin
4 Cedar of Lebanon
5 Wild flower lawn
6 Terraces
7 Oak
8 Copper beeches
9 Dogwoods
10 Meconopsis garden
11 Fountain
12 Plane tree
13 The weeping oak
14 Islands with castle-ruin follies
15 Mixed woodland – planted 1969

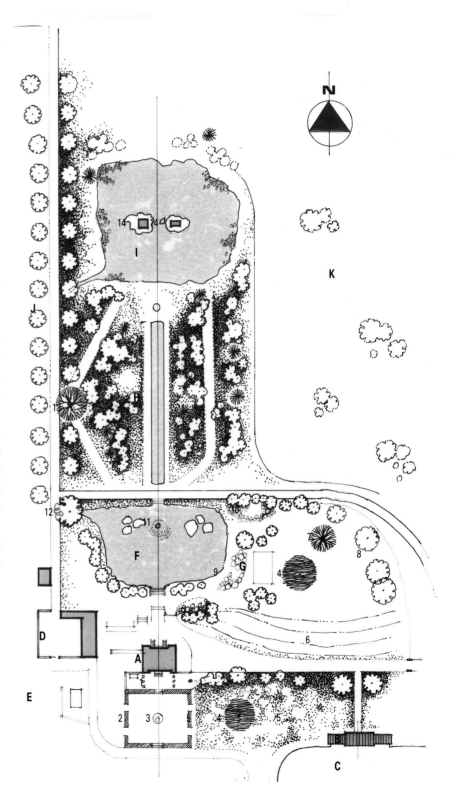

19

20

Greatly extending the size of a low, naturally fed farm pond by excavation, George Clive created an attractive lake. He used the excavated earth to make islands on which, using old stone from demolition sites, he built impressive folly ruins which command the attention of anyone standing on the terrace in the front of the house

he began to gain confidence as a mason. Next, he hired a contractor with a mechanical digger to clean out the pond and raise its status to that of a small lake; Clive then realised that the capacity of such diggers is so great that anyone with the land available could become his own Capability Brown.

It has turned out to be a wonderfully fruitful discovery. At a lower level still was an area of flat and boggy meadowland simply begging for improvement. The answer, which wouldn't have occurred to a more conventional gardener, was to bring in the contractor again to dig a straight canal into the clay subsoil – 90 yards long, 20 feet wide and 5 feet deep. He then flanked it with Siberian iris, blue hardy geranium and orange and red Leopard lilies; made simple flanking paths and planted beech and larch with a variety of birches, including pinkish-silvery barked *Betula ermanii*, and added the dazzling white barked *B. jacquemontii* for more sparkle. Limes, horse chestnuts and wild cherries were also planted to strengthen the matrix and increase the interest of these lateral plantations.

To draw the eye down the canal he positioned an over-life-sized eighteenth-century figure of a warrior with child on a pedestal at its end. And for most latter-day Versailles-makers that would have been enough. But Clive was so pleased with what he had done ('for little more than it would have cost to buy a modest car at the time') that he couldn't resist doing more.

Both the top pond and the canal had to be fed by pumping from another small natural pond on even lower land beyond the canal which collected water from springs and natural drainage. This, George Clive realised, offered an opportunity for an even more ambitious water feature. Bringing back the digging contractor yet again, he deepened and enlarged the feeder pond until it became a 1½ acre lake. Much of the spill from the excavation was used to create two islands high enough to be seen clearly from the house. They provided an ideal site on which to build a folly from old stone window surrounds and mullioning recovered from demolished buildings. From the lake shore it is impossible to imagine that it is anything other than a medieval ruin.

Clive then realised he could draw the eye even further into the landscape. He was fortunate in owning a hedge on rising ground several hundred yards from the far margin of the lake. By removing a few trees from it he was able to open up a vista of beautiful hills many miles beyond, so that from the house door one can look down along the canal, past the statue to the lake with its folly, and then on into the Herefordshire countryside.

At the same time as excavating and building, George Clive did not ignore the need for attractive planting. He paid great attention to the area round the top pond where displays could be enjoyed from the door of the house. There he planted a large number of ornamental trees including the exotic flowering Magnolias *M. kobus*, *M. salicifolia*, and *M. veitchii*, *Zelkova serrata*

whose leaves turn bronze red in autumn, as well as oaks, cedars, Scots pine and sweet chestnut.

In another part of the garden, beyond the north-east edge of the upper pond, George Clive has devoted a large area to a solid bed of Meconopsis poppies. There, in their season, such beauties as the bright red *M. napaulensis*, the blue *M. betonicifolia*, the gentian *M. grandis*, the yellow nodding *M. chelidonifolia* and the purple and white *M. horridula* display their wonderfully transparent papery petals.

To increase the interest of a walk through the established woodlands he has enriched the path edges with lilies, a variety of acers, rowans and white beams.

Almost as if to prove that the habit of tinkering with the landscape can become addictive, George Clive has more recently started to beautify the banks of a fishing pond which can only be seen when driving from the gates of the estate to the house. It will be interesting to see what he does next.

The smooth lawn on the lower terrace to the south of the house is separated from the lovely wooded parkland at Whitfield by a hedge embellished with topiary work. At its heart there's a basin feature which George Clive created by restoring seventeenth- and eighteenth-century relics

TREVOR CRUMP

IN MINIATURE

It took a long time for Australian designers to break free from many of the conventions which dictated the garden style of their European – notably British – forebears. But now that they have done so and have learned to take a justifiable pride in their separate identity they have produced a vernacular of their own along with a host of gardens which are as exciting and original in concept as any to be seen in the world. And these days, instead of producing designs which really depend for their success on the subdued and misty light and essentially maritime climate of northern Europe they have opted for schemes wholly appropriate to their own environment. On the whole they have stressed the clean lines and bold statements of form which read so well in a light of astonishing luminescence against iridescent skies of the intensest blue.

While realising that, given the water which modern irrigation systems are capable of providing, just about anything can be grown in a Sydney suburb, they have increasingly turned to their own native flora in order to give their designs a particular identity.

This is the design philosophy which has increasingly dominated the work of the outstanding Sydney landscaper Trevor Crump, whose best work, like that of contemporary garden architects elsewhere, inevitably results from the challenge offered by small plots in urban and suburban situations.

The garden which Crump made to front and back a house in the Woolhara suburb of Sydney offers an inspiring example of what can be achieved on a small plot by a talented designer.

Apart from something of outstanding aesthetic appeal, his client's main requirements were for a very low-maintenance garden with the emphasis on facilities for outdoor living in a warm climate.

The main feature in the back garden (see plan) – occupying the last third of its area – is a spectacular and elegant square summerhouse on a raised mound reached by mounting a double flight of steps from the lower lawn area. Its screening walls are made of tight trellis work above brick pierced by round *oeil de boeuf* 'windows' which offer vistas both inside and outside the garden.

The roof consists of solid structural timbers with no cladding and open access to the sky. But as the garden matures they give support to climbers planted to offer shade from Sydney's burning summer sun.

The trellis is painted in the palest of blues with the brick and other vertical features picked out in another pastel blue of a slightly darker tone. These surfaces contrast strikingly with a bold floor of large black and white ceramic tiles arranged in a diamond pattern.

A pair of pot-grown Australian native 'Black Boy' plants were chosen by Trevor Crump as guardians to stand before the house door into the paved front yard of a house in Sydney

TREVOR CRUMP: Garden Plan

A House
B Front Terrace
C Entrance
D Balcony
E Summer house

1 Black boys in pots
2 Palm
3 Steps up to first floor
4 Lawn
5 Citrus trees
6 Wall with buttresses
7 Steps down
8 Gravel path
9 Cypress

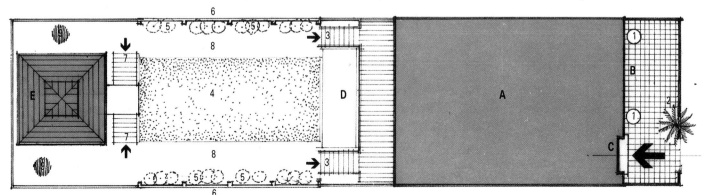

An elegant timber frame and trellis summerhouse dominates Trevor Crump's design for this back garden. Evergreen citrus trees planted in the alcoves between the supporting columns of the lateral walls prevent the masonry from seeming too dominant

24

Seen from the house, flanked by a pair of pencil cypresses, in its economy of line and the restraint of its surrounding planting, this building has the simplicity and appeal of a tiny fishermen's chapel overlooking the sea on an Aegean island. But people enjoying its shelter aren't deprived of this pleasurable view because the architect and the landscaper have collaborated and arranged for the house windows giving onto the ground and first floor balconies at the other end of the lawn to have mirrored surfaces which reflect back the image of the summerhouse.

To contrast with the blue sparkle of the summerhouse, there is a restful tablet of close-mown lawn edged by gravel walks. These are lined by young citrus trees set in the alcoves between the piers of the side walls. It is all very simple, formal and elegant with the weekly lawn-clip and picking the fruit as the only serious work burdens.

On the street-front of the house even less work is involved. The garden there consists of a simple rectangular court paved with the same bold diamonds of black and white ceramic tiles which are used to floor the summerhouse. A large palm has been planted to shade the area and on each side of the front door Trevor Crump has stationed two pot-grown 'black boys'. These are tousleheaded Australian native plants which, when their foliage is badly charred in bush fires, stand out among the scorched desolation like startled golliwogs. It is another of those Australian plants whose seeds need cooking below an underbrush fire before they will germinate.

Like all good designers, Trevor Crump has evolved in this scheme a very simple theme and used it throughout the garden. Having decided to use trellis of a particularly attractive kind as walls for his summerhouse, he has adopted the same material to make railings for both the balconies on the house and for the banisters to the steps leading up to the first floor, giving an obvious and very pleasing feeling of continuity.

PIETRO PORCINAI

LOVE IN A HOT CLIMATE

'Look – it is wonderful,' commanded Professor Pietro Porcinai as the tip of his finger caressed the mirror-black surface of the water in the central stone basin of the nymphaeum adjoining his studio in Fiesole.

Outside the temperature was in the nineties and still rising. Down below in the valley the Arno was just an oily streak and Florence had almost vanished in the milky midday haze; harsh conditions, to alleviate which a comfort-craving Medici prince had the nymphaeum in the grounds of his summer palace built by Bernardo Buontalenti. Visitors to the palace during the burning Tuscan summers must certainly have found welcome relief from the heat in its cool damp air and from the sun's brightness in its almost sepulchral light, for the great, vaulted, windowless chamber is lit only by small occuli which pierce its roof. The scant greenish light which they admit is reflected by the surfaces of the water features and by the shiny mother-of-pearl insides of the thousands of seashells which encrust the vault.

The lazy wake developing as Porcinai's finger trailed over the surface of the basin rocked the image of the occulus above, beaming it back towards the wall of the vault, making the shells glitter like tiger's eyes. 'That's what I mean,' he proclaimed. 'No element is as capable as water

of inducing a change of mood so quickly. One moment it is calm and placid, the next it's all excited animation.' He nodded towards the extravaganza which made up the end wall of the nymphaeum where water raced over a rocky escarpment past sculptured figures before tumbling into another stone basin.

Porcinai, who was lovingly restoring the nymphaeum, was one of the world's great masters when it came to the use of water in gardens. That is why architect Oscar Niemeyer asked him to create a water feature round a factory in Milan which would render a water-storage tower superfluous, and why so many wealthy Italian and Middle Eastern clients commissioned him to establish gardens with prominent water features in the grounds of their villas.

Porcinai couldn't understand how anyone could be happy in a garden which lacked water in some form, 'because it is one of the four major elements into which man first classified the world, but in many gardens it is the missing element and this prevents them from becoming what they should be – a true microcosm of the world beyond.'

The chief importance of water in garden design, apart from its reassuring presence as a sustainer of life, is, he contended, 'that it exposes the perceptions to a whole new series of experiences. When calm, it reflects the colour and constantly changing character of the sky. In movement – gently splashing down from jets or fountains, racing over weirs or gurgling over rocks – it can sing, soothe or excite. And, because it reflects light, it can be valuable, too, in luring the eye deep into the garden, beckoning visitors to explore further. Channelled into streams or canals it can also be used to greatly extend vistas.'

Often working in warm climates, Porcinai inevitably attracted clients anxious to have swimming pools in their gardens. These are frequently obtrusive features which disturb what might otherwise be a very natural-feeling design; often the attendant buildings – the engine- and filter-house or the changing rooms – cause the greatest

Sweet-water canals alongside the swimming pool provide homes for aquatic plants in this garden by Pietro Porcinai near Florence. He used ivies climbing on wire frames to create quick shady arbours

offence. At the Villa Palmieri near Florence, Porcinai overcame this problem by simply burying all the buildings beneath a huge bank of soil planted with a thick stand of the attractive black-stemmed dwarf bamboo *Arundinaria nigra* to produce a sloping, high-level lawn. He also used one of his favourite ploys here – confining a channel of fresh water alongside and apparently contiguous with the water in the swimming pool. With bold papyrus, water lilies and other aquatic plants established in fresh water, bathers can easily imagine that they are swimming in a natural, flower-filled lake.

At another villa located on the spine of a promontory near Portofino, more than 300 feet above sea level, Porcinai contrived a pool in which both the bathers and people watching them from the house terrace can imagine that they are actually swimming in the sea. On its outer edge the pool has no visual barrier to mark the division between the surface of its water and that of the sea far below. Instead of being held back by a vertical barrier, a thin film of water is allowed to flow continuously over the outer edge of the pool as it would over a weir. Having fallen

By making the outer margin of this pool into a weir over which water continually trickles, Pietro Porcinai created the impression that its surface was contiguous with that of the sea more than 100 feet below

PIETRO PORCINAI: Pool Section

1 Pool
2 Pool terrace
3 Pumping chamber
4 Water to pool
5 Over flow to provide raised water edge
6 Cascade
7 Collecting channel
8 Drainage pipe
9 Collecting cistern
10 Connecting pipe 'pump to cistern'

29

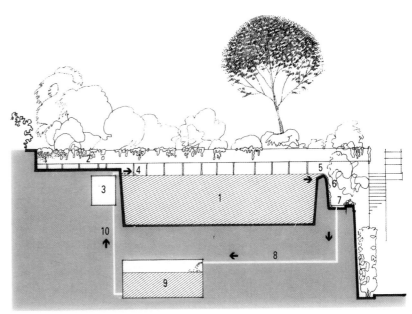

over the outer wall the water is then channelled via a gurgling stream back to the pump which is housed in a chamber excavated into the rock for recirculation to the pool. It is an audacious work made all the more credible because while excavating the pool Porcinai decided to leave large rocks which protruded into the line of its outer margin in place and to incorporate them into the pool's design.

Even when he couldn't introduce such natural features, Porcinai tried to integrate pools into the landscape. Rather than use chrome-railed external steps to allow access to a pool, he favoured modelling its floor to create underwater steps or a gentle entrance ramp. He refused to countenance diving boards or unsightly apparatus to enable the pool to be covered. Only under exceptional circumstances would he consider specifying a blue lining for his pools; he felt that it looked unnatural in a garden. Instead he preferred to use a matt black lining which would turn the pool into a mirror of the sky and surrounding vegetation and provide the most natural effect of all – the floors of most ponds and lakes are dark. Sometimes, instead of black linings he used locally obtained pebbles set in concrete if he felt that they would be more appropriate to the rest of his design.

In Professor Porcinai's opinion, Burle Marx in Brazil, Isamon Noguchi in the USA, Geoffrey Jellicoe, Brenda Colvine and Russell Page in Britain and Cecil Pinsant, an Englishman working in Florence before the war, were among the most stylish of twentieth-century garden designers. In their work they all manifested that gift of style which, he believed, comes about only if everything in the immediate environment of the garden is taken fully into consideration. This includes such factors as the quality of the light and the most frequent colour and mood of the sky, the geology and vegetation of both the site and the region, the appearance and materials of the surrounding buildings and the scale of the most obvious features. However, Porcinai acknowledged that a designer *could* pay due attention to all these features and produce a fine and acceptable garden without that distinguishing extra, which observers recognise as style.

'That is possessed only by works which, from the moment they are completed, will influence the work of other designers,' he explained, pointing out that he didn't mean that a work of style would start anything as superficial as a fashion. But, rather, that it would influence the spirit in which later designers would approach their projects. He was equally certain that style has rarely resulted from projects where a patron was unduly influential or where town planning committees were involved. Since he frequently became involved in large-scale works involving substantial changes to land contours in urban areas (often lifting levels to improve vistas), he inevitably came into conflict with town planning departments who would interfere by applying building or planning regulations.

'Style only ever seems to emerge from interpreters working alone,' he explained. 'While happy to listen to the requirements of my clients during an initial briefing, I refuse to accept work unless they understand that, from that moment onwards, I am totally in command and make all the decisions on the project.'

The professor was pessimistic about the future of really stylish large-scale work because he had noticed an increase in the amount of official interference wherever he had worked over the past twenty years. 'It is difficult to achieve beautiful things whilst having to spend so much time complying with the unreasonable demands of what often appear to be jealous men of little understanding or talent whose aim seems to be more to frustrate than encourage.'

Despite this constraint on liberty, Professor Porcinai overcame the authorities on many occasions, a fine example being the garden which he created for a villa on the spine of a hill outside Florence. There he had to work on a triangular site in the fork of two roads. While the view from the terrace of the house (which was built on a mound) stretched away over the valleys on either side of the spine, the garden area was much lower and the view greatly restricted. Asked to rectify the situation, Porcinai wanted to retain the good features of the garden: a well-established hedge of evergreen oaks closely planted along each arm of the road fork, and several mature trees. His solution was to raise the level of the garden just inside the hedge by, in places, up to twenty feet. He supported the new high terrace garden on several small and one large central brick cupolas, thus creating one of the world's most elegant underground car parks. With space for a dozen cars, it has the atmosphere of a Byzantine church rather than of a garage, and has already served as the venue for a 'society' ball.

The coffered ceiling makes a variety of depths of soil available for planting on the high terrace (or roof garden) above. The deep pockets, where the domes of the cupolas dip down in to their supporting columns, provide fine homes for large trees, while the shallow areas over the tops of the cupolas support less demanding plants.

Since a parking area needs good ventilation, the tops of the cupolas are open to the sky and protected by beautiful iron 'lanterns'. The outer walls of the parking area are pierced by large oval *oeil de boeuf* vents through which the straight dark stems of the original holm oak

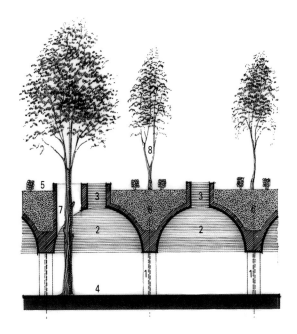

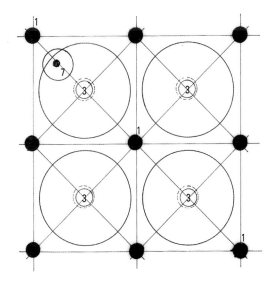

31

PIETRO PORCINAI: Villa: Florence. Raised garden level. Garage lower level

1 Column supports with drainage
2 Brick cupolas
3 Ventilation lanterns
4 Lower garage level
5 Upper garden level
6 Planting areas
7 Large vents for large existing trees
8 Planting on upper level to suit soil depths available

hedge can be seen against the bright Florentine light, creating a magical atmosphere.

Wherever a mature tree in the garden deserved preservation, Porcinai allowed it to grow unmolested beneath the floor of the parking area, simply pruning main branches from the trunk until it emerged through a hole created for it in the roof above. To prevent accidents, the gap between the trunks and the edge of the surrounding exit ports was floored with open ironwork.

On the terrace above the car park, Porcinai created a large and dignified *parterre* using clipped box shapes to divide a pattern of brick-topped walkways (with shady areas under the canopy of trees) from swatches of soothing emerald lawn (see photograph left). This is a garden of pleasing and deceptive simplicity – in perfect harmony with the noble but plain façade of the house – providing a promenade with some of the finest views in Europe.

It is interesting to note that Porcinai chose to use brick cupolas to support his terrace rather than the more usual reinforced concrete: 'because this ancient technique, with all the hand labour involved, now turns out to be cheaper.' The man, whose clients included some of the richest people in Europe and who charged fees commensurate with the grandeur of the schemes he offered, found that discovery highly amusing. But, like all good designers, he wasn't irresponsibly spendthrift: he just didn't want the execution of brilliant ideas to be thwarted by lack of finance. When appropriate, he often adopted cheap solutions.

Near a pool in Fiesole, he has brilliantly adapted an eighteenth-century idea: ivy crawling over a beehive-shaped frame of iron rods has grown into a dense canopy which shades a circular seat. It's a lovely way of producing a stylish living feature quickly. 'Ideal for a tête à tête,' Porcinai explained with a gleam in his eye.

It is easy to make a leafy bower very quickly by planting ivies to grow on a frame made from steel bars and galvanised wire netting

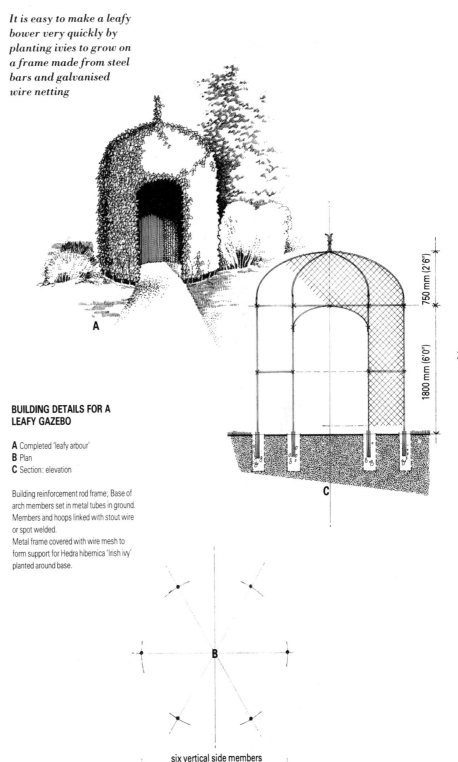

BUILDING DETAILS FOR A LEAFY GAZEBO

A Completed 'leafy arbour'
B Plan
C Section: elevation

Building reinforcement rod frame; Base of arch members set in metal tubes in ground. Members and hoops linked with stout wire or spot welded.
Metal frame covered with wire mesh to form support for Hedra hibernica 'Irish ivy' planted around base.

750 mm (2'6")

1800 mm (6'0")

six vertical side members
2100 mm (7'0")

33

DAVID HICKS

INSPIRATION IN DETAIL

No contemporary garden designer has a stronger belief in the importance of style than David Hicks, as his use of phrases such as 'design with deliberation' will attest. He has a powerful understanding of the historical period over which gardening styles have evolved, and points out that, in earlier centuries, gardening was preoccupied with line and form, though formality was sometimes carried to excess. In the eighteenth century gardens became much more informal as curves and the 'picturesque' swept everything else aside. Eventually, the Victorian English garden with its herbaceous borders and beds set the style all over the world. Now that most gardens are smaller than those of the past, David Hicks believes that the advantages of the more formally planned and structured garden are once more being recognised.

It would be a mistake to deduce from this that Hicks stamps *his* style on all the gardens he designs. In fact, he has great respect for other people's sense of style, although, he says, 'it is foolish simply to imitate. I freely admit that the best of ideas in my own garden are adapted from those of other people whose taste I admire. But I have never attempted exactly to reproduce someone else's solution.' What is so special about a David Hicks garden is the sensitivity with which he uses the elements available, thus revealing 'the spirit of the place.'

Undoubtedly, the fact that David Hicks is an interior designer has had a profound influence on his particular development as a gardener. He admits that he has always been attracted to gardens that have a strong sense of containment, not dissimilar to rooms. He admires 'sheltered areas with apertures leading excitingly on to other areas,' of which the obvious examples are Hidcote and Sissinghurst. 'A sense of surprise can be achieved by creating outdoor rooms,' he says: 'Surprise, contrast, not seeing everything at once – these are the elements that give me pleasure.'

Hicks' leaning towards structure rather than informality is never given undue emphasis in the gardens he has designed or developed. Rather, the hallmark of his style is the brilliance with which he attends to detail and to what might seem to be the less dramatic elements of the design. Here are a few examples of his approach:

Every detail of the garden must be decisive. The design of the entrance gate, the colour of the gravel on the drive, the colour and texture of the brick and mortar used for the walls – all must be related. These boundaries and divisions are vitally important; like the binding of a book, they are the handsome externals which announce a well-presented interior.

Strive for variety of texture and material underfoot. This is going to be significant through-

A very unusual stone fountain has been designed, surrounded by flint. Above the lion's head is David Hicks' tribute to his mother-in-law, Countess Mountbatten of Burma

35

out the year, whatever the season. Some of the best gardens rely principally on texture for their effect – contrasting a hard line of flagstones with the softer but still sculptural lines of clipped hedges, or contrasting large-leafed plants with the tighter 'weave' of box behind. Texture should be designed into a garden. The drama of bare branches against a winter sky may be as striking as full foliage in spring and summer. An example of textural contrast given by David Hicks is a summer tapestry of hosta, iris, thistle and crambe against a yew hedge. At his own home he was lucky enough to find, under a thin layer of concrete in the back yard, several thousand cobblestones which he re-used as a surround to the swimming pool to contrast with the water, and as a border round his front-door porch.

The colour of doors and gates (and even such things as the wheelbarrow) should be carefully considered. David Hicks favours a dark green paint for doors, tubs and seats. White-painted furniture has, he feels, become rather a cliché and he suggests buffs, beiges and other subtle colours be considered.

The siting of garden seats and ornaments is crucial. Before building a brick base for a container, for example, lay the bricks out dry. Then place the container on the base and wait three or four weeks to see if it still looks right – both the height and the overall proportions of the base can be changed if necessary.

Instead of the conventional standard bay trees and roses, try other standard plants in tubs – for example, *Hydrangea paniculata* in standard form, and honeysuckle. Other possibilities include standard gooseberries or shaped may trees in large Versailles tubs or in pots.

These are just a few of Hicks' pointers on putting gardening ideas to practical effect. It would be wrong to conclude, though, that all his detailed work is the result of carefully considered planning; sometimes there will be an imaginative leap forward as the result of an accidental discovery. For example, he recalls how he once made a most successful ornament from the old obelisk-shaped lightning conductor from Blenheim which he discovered in a builder's yard. David Hicks believes in encouraging the accidental. In planning a new garden, he says, always allow the element of human error to creep into the most formal of approaches. This gives a certain warmth to what could otherwise be too austere. He asks: 'Consider how far-off trees, which may not have been deliberately planned to be in place, when peeping over enclosed areas give an excitement and a dimension to the garden as well as prompting the thought "What is over there?"' It is perhaps the essence of David Hicks' work that he combines a cool, traditional formalism with a most extraordinary sense of surprise.

His own garden in Oxfordshire surrounds what was formally the dower-house belonging to the much larger house in which he first lived. The dower-house had been converted into a farm, and the old brick walls and farm buildings still surrounded it, as did a large number of fine old trees. Less than ten years ago he set about reconstructing the garden area, virtually starting from scratch to replace the neglected gardens, refurbishing the one existing lawn, and adding what are now splendid new lawns. From his former garden he moved some plants – choisyas, hellebores, bergenia, *Iris stylosa*, hydrangeas, honeysuckles and acanthus – as well as old roses, although he also acquired many more from plantsmen and nurseries.

It is a medium-sized garden which gives the impression of being large and varied because of the skill with which Hicks has reconstructed its various components. To the left of the south garden is an area of grass surrounded on three sides by an arched walk made of standard commercial frames in plastic-covered metal (which will eventually disappear beneath the foliage). They are bedded in concrete below the top-soil. The interesting aspect of this tunnel walk is that the plants and trees which cover the frames are a mixture of roses – including Cli Ophelia, Zepherine Drouhin, Lady Hillingdon, La Reine Victoria and Lady Waterlow – mixed with clematis, honeysuckle, passion flower, jasmine, wistaria, hornbeam, willow and sweet chestnut to give winter body. This leads into the main south garden beyond the lawn in front of the house which is made up of clipped hornbeam trees with hornbeam hedges under and slightly behind them. At the end of the lines of hornbeam is a *clairvoyce* which David Hicks made by taking down a wide area of the original wall. Near the house these hornbeams open out into 'wings' which edge the small lawn on its upper level. He removed two mature evergreens, a yew and a cypress, so that the lawn could sweep freely up from its lower level in front of the house to the raised area above.

To the right, at the upper level, is an enclosed line of hazel trees which can be walked *round*, rather than through – another 'room'. This in turn leads through a door in the wall into a further 'room'. Its main feature was constructed by turning what was previously a long, low cow shed into a raised terrace. About three feet above the level of the garden, this terrace was built out of old stones and cobbles discovered in the cow shed and where the farmyard had been. Behind it, in the centre of the fine brick wall, a small water spout trickles into a stone trough. In front of the terraces, on the lawns, are two lines of pleached limes.

DAVID HICKS: West Garden Plan

A House
B Long barn
C Tall barn
D Pool
E Raised terrace: pots and plants

1 Lawn
2 Sloping grass ramp
3 Gravel path
4 Sunken gravel path
5 Clipped chestnuts: underplanted with aesculus hedging
6 Urn

7 Clipped may trees
8 Stone paved terrace
9 Tulips followed by lilies and nicotianas
10 Box
11 Pleached limes
12 Stone wall
13 Water feature

14 Beds of lavender set in cobble stones
15 Large pots on brick plinths
16 Long grass (cut twice a year)
17 Chestnut avenue
18 Grass land: horses and sheep
19 Gravel-surfaced yard

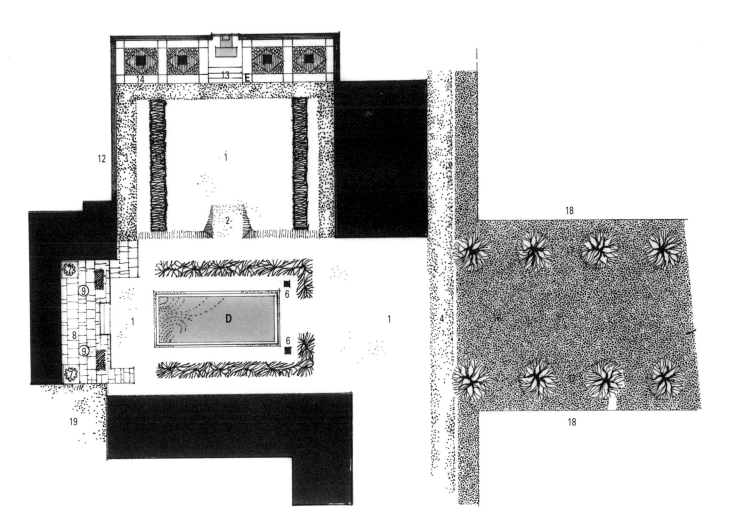

The terrace is dotted with an assortment of urns and large terracotta pots, filled with lilies, all-white, pink and yellow. 'The difficulty with these,' says David Hicks, 'is that they cannot face our very severe winters. I am a great believer in pots, even if they are too big to move, but the plants really ought to be brought into shelter before the frosts.'

Behind this garden is what must be called the Great Vista. Starting from the house one sees first of all the long swimming pool. What began as its black lining has now weathered into a most attractive lapis-lazuli. On either side is a row of chestnut trees, which were clipped five years after being planted, and beneath them, a chestnut hedge: 'Probably the only one in the world,' says Hicks with due modesty. Beyond the tree-lined pool area is another lawn bounded by a gravel path. The eye sweeps along the length of the pool, beyond the gravel path, and is led up a further line of chestnut trees and on through another *clairvoyce* on the edge of the farmland, perhaps 200 yards from the house. Further on still, on the most distant edge of the farmland, at the 'horizon', tall trees have been taken down to make yet another focal point where the sky opens beyond them. It is magnificent and, it must be admitted, only possible for someone with several hundred acres of farmland surrounding his or her garden. But how few gardeners would have turned the possible into practical effect?

One of the gardens is called the 'herbaceous', although it is far from conventional in terms of planting. First, the beds themselves are cut in a 'key' pattern, so the effect is of a series of formal shapes filled with an apparent informality of plants. Then, apart from the crambe, very few of the usual herbaceous clichés feature: there is much acanthus and many hostas; a honeysuckle climbs up a tapering tripod of wood; other plants include sedums, hydrangeas, pinks, lilies, cordifolia, daphnes, and peace roses.

This garden is not 'herbaceous' in the now commonly accepted sense of a mass of colour, although it conforms to the correct sense of the word as 'dying down every year'.

Elsewhere in his garden, David Hicks is making valiant efforts to grow magnolia. The harsh winters of recent years mean that these have to be protected by wooden structures (painted the required green) if they are to be brought into flower. 'Like Queen Victoria, who longed to be brought a ripe mango from her garden, I long to bring magnolias into the house,' says David Hicks.

His original ideas apply just as much to the house inside as outside. For example, he will arrange cut gypsophila as a standard tree on a straight cherry stem for the winter. Herbs, when they are burgeoning at the awkward time for flowers between the beginning of May and the middle of June, can be arrayed as either one variety alone in a vase, or as a mixed collection. Another David Hicks original is to grow sunflowers in a wild area, cut them late in September and early October, and make an arrangement of them in a huge bucket on the floor. A final example: when rhubarb begins to go to seed, cut it when it looks at its most primeval, before it bursts, and bring it indoors. David Hicks' rhubarb is not grown in some obscure corner of the garden but in a series of bold metre-square beds which he has cut along the length of a lime-tree walk.

David Hicks is called a 'new formalist' because of his liking for planned and structural gardens, but the term must not be taken to imply that he has a dry or mannered style. There is a side to his work which is romantic, almost fantastic, and, like all good stylists, he defies classification.

*A perfectly symmetrical
pool set in a svelte lawn
uncluttered by
disturbing pool
paraphernalia and
flanked by chestnut
allées demonstrates just
how pleasing a formal
treatment of a relatively
small garden area
can be*

39

THE SPENCERS

EXERCISING CONTROL

When Sybil Spencer and her late husband Frederick of York Gate, Adel near Leeds bought what was, in 1951, a bleak grey stone farmhouse, the land about it, she recollects, was hardly a promising prospect. But a derelict orchard, comprising three old apple trees and a pear, was exactly the sort of challenge which real gardeners love. 'The one great advantage was that there was a good flat patch behind the house from which the land then sloped down towards a stream.'

Frederick and Sybil Spencer's first moves were to lay down the broad outlines of their intended landscape. An extensive fruit and vegetable garden was established behind the house, with a second vegetable plot on a lower slope to one side. In front of the house they built a terrace and used a stream immediately below it to feed a water garden. Elsewhere, new shrubs and trees were interspersed with bulbs and herbaceous plants in order to divert attention from their immaturity.

When Frederick Spencer died, the design work was taken over by his son Robin, a surveyor whose skill with masonry and garden architecture can have been equalled only rarely. In his tragically short working life he disposed tens of tons of cobblestones, gravel and rock into contours of impeccable taste and style. His setting of the plants at Adel was more beautiful and

sympathetic than that achieved by many of the most gifted landscapers of his epoch.

The hub of his design is an ingenious cobblestone and gravel maze near the garden's low entrance, from which pathways ascend the garden in intriguing patterns of cobbles, slabs and cracked stone. With total assurance he used elements which might have appeared harsh, to produce soft and intriguing features.

A notable example of Robin Spencer's ability

This grass allée (so described because its paving is flanked by grass) at York Gate is less than 20 yards long. But the proportions of its width and the height of its boundary hedges were chosen with such care that it seems much longer

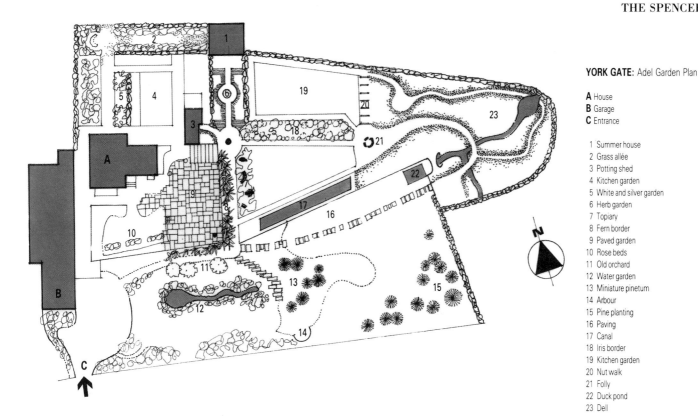

A House
B Garage
C Entrance

1 Summer house
2 Grass allée
3 Potting shed
4 Kitchen garden
5 White and silver garden
6 Herb garden
7 Topiary
8 Fern border
9 Paved garden
10 Rose beds
11 Old orchard
12 Water garden
13 Miniature pinetum
14 Arbour
15 Pine planting
16 Paving
17 Canal
18 Iris border
19 Kitchen garden
20 Nut walk
21 Folly
22 Duck pond
23 Dell

to bring about the delicate visual counterpoint which is evident in all his work is a path between deep, solid beds of pastel-shaded irises which is edged with cobblestones and has a repeated pattern of diamonds made from cobbles set between the edges. The gaps between the cobble patterns are filled with coarse gravel. The points of the diamonds are echoed by the spiky iris leaves; the way in which the gravel fragments the light is taken up by the delicate haze of the flowers.

The broad gravelled walk through the white garden might have appeared bleak and featureless were it not for the way Spencer punctuated its surface with a central line of solid stepping stones formed by setting large stone grinding wheels into it at regular intervals.

In a rich small pinetum which his mother planted with an attractive range of smallish conifers, he covered the ground with a layer of very large, well-rounded river pebbles. This makes a wonderful contrast to the planted beds, the formal pathways and mown grass walks, and is the perfect natural background for the colourful, prickly-looking conifer foliage.

The ability to exploit fully the characteristics of particular plants is evident everywhere in the Spencers' garden, but it is demonstrated most memorably in an enchanting herb garden. Confined within an alley between two very tall, tightly clipped yew hedges, it is best enjoyed from a fine Italianate summerhouse where Virgil himself would have felt at home. From here one can peer down a central gravelled path, across a wider circular area halfway down its length (which features a giant millstone), and on through a portal piercing an end 'wall' of clipped yew, emphasised by a pair of large yew topiary balls sited above its flanks. The form of these balls is mirrored in low rows of spherical golden box planted on either side of the path, which also serve to accentuate its line. In their season, the large globular umbels of ornamental alliums planted among the herbs in the beds between the path and the hedges recapitulate the theme. Two

Above: *Stone grinding wheels were used to relieve the monotony of a gravel path through the silver and white garden at York Gate*

Right: *View from beneath the loggia of the Roman summerhouse at York Gate along the herb garden.*

tall corkscrew clipped spires of *Buxus semper-virens* provide a smart contrast and prevent the theme from becoming too obvious or repetitive.

The spherical motif is used elsewhere in the garden and its recurrence in different materials, as on the stone finials at the corners of walls, helps give a certain unity to the different areas. It is used most effectively in a spherical stone sundial set on top of a high corkscrew-carved stone column which acts as the focal point of the vista

down the path between the beds in the white garden. This subtle appreciation of the nuances of garden geometry is what makes a visit to Adel such a rewarding experience.

Equally satisfying but more rustic effects have been obtained by cutting and training hazels to form a tunnelled nut walk, whilst a circular, open-topped temple folly has been created from ancient roof timbers clad with wistaria.

Throughout the garden the pathways are

Far right: Bold, rounded beach pebbles are here used very successfully to mulch the ground in the dwarf conifer bed. Their curved shapes contrast splendidly with the spikiness of the conifer foliage

aligned to emphasize vistas and exaggerate the sense of distance. And in one case the effect has been amplified by flanking a path with a waist-high water-lily canal contained within splendid, bold stone-block walls.

In spite of the presence of many formal garden features, the aim has been to retain a cottage-garden atmosphere appropriate for the farmhouse which the garden surrounds. To this end, most of the objects used for ornament are utilitarian, such as stone troughs and sinks, stone grinding wheels and mill stones, iron pump heads, old boilers and even large, old kitchen pans.

A similar attitude has been adopted towards the planting, which in general is suitably billowy and profuse. But few cottage gardeners would have selected material of such rarity and used it with such sophisticated taste. Not many of them, for example, would have sought out variegated sweet chestnuts, or quite so many varieties of fern. Nor would many have dreamt of planting yuccas, trilliums, ornamental grasses of many types, and several species of arum lily including *A. italicum* 'Pictum', *A. creticum*, *A. dioscoridis* and *A. orientalis*. Several rare and spiky New Zealand aciphyllas also provoke comment among a planting designed to provide colour at either end of the season and two or even three successions of bloom from the same patch of land.

Perhaps the most unexpected sight of all is the Atlantic cedar which would normally grow to become a huge parasol of a tree but which at Adel is espaliered along a wall with enormous branches spreading out from a hefty mainstream which is only 5 feet tall. Sybil Spencer says they decided to espalier it just to see what would happen. The result is astonishing and demonstrates once again that a major requirement in garden design is the ability to exercise control.

This garden is only rarely open to the public under the National Gardens Scheme – see that organisation's annual list for details.

The gravel maze near the low entrance at York Gate serves as an intriguing starting point for paths which lead up into several different areas of the garden

John Stefanidis

THE SPIRIT OF THE PLACE

What can you do when you find that one of the most beautiful views in the south of England is best seen from a vantage point surrounded on all sides by a group of cow sheds? This was the problem facing John Stefanidis, one of the most stylish interior designers in the country, but the single-level house with extensions that he evolved from the cow sheds has such immediate charm that any reference to its origins seems almost in bad taste.

At first sight, the interior appears to be a very comfortable work of art rather than something produced by an architect or craftsman. The designer's hand has been so subtly at work and everything looks so completely natural that the extent of the work done would not be generally realised. There are no parquet floors here, but bricks which might have been trampled on by cows, although in fact they were carefully chosen and laid. Other details are taken from the building's original function as a cow shed, such as the slatted covers on the windows that condition the light and make the outward views balance the inward ones, extending the range of the house so that at times the house and garden seem one.

We are here to talk about the garden, not the house, and indeed it is the garden which makes the first and most lasting impression on the visitor. You drive up a narrow country lane, advance through a wide and unremarkable country gate, and park in a long, low, open brick-and-wood farm building which was probably where the farmer kept his hay cart or, later, his tractors. The inner wall of this building contains a door, flanked, it is true, by two tubs of Portuguese laurel, but that is no preparation for what is going to strike you when you open the door. You are standing in another low, open building, but you are no longer in England. You are no longer in a country farmyard. You are in a new world.

The loggia in which you find yourself is a spacious area in which to sit and survey the scene ahead – a courtyard bounded on all sides by the low walls of the house. The courtyard is about one-half formal orchard, and one-half a large box *parterre* of an unusual and somewhat complex design. You seat yourself in one of the comfortable wicker chairs in the loggia and look around. It is a long, gravel-floored, open-fronted building, based on the original farm building but now filled with large terracotta pots arranged in a rather formal way. Hostas behind, and in front six white agapanthus, their pots standing on a low brick base to raise them above the lawn, which runs ahead for about 25 yards. On either side of the lawn is a tall yew hedge, and down the centre a stone path. This area is the formal orchard, made up of ten apple trees to the left of the path and ten to the right. They are of several varieties, and their branches will eventually be

This striking feature made from drums of cut flints set in concrete and separated by bracelets of old brick was deliberately placed to one side of the main axis through the courtyard garden to prevent the garden's otherwise perfect symmetry from becoming too boring

JOHN STEFANIDIS:
Courtyard Garden Plan

A Long low brick and wood open farm building: part car park, part storage.
B Loggia: gravel floor
C House
D Guest cottage
E Courtyard: half formal orchard, half large box parterre
F Small garden
G Secret garden
H Herb garden

1 Entrance with 2 pots
2 Stone path
3 Apple trees in lawn
4 Yew hedge
5 'Windows' cut in hedge
6 Metal arches with trained apple trees
7 Flint and brick pillar: 8'0" high
8 Gravel path and areas
9 Box parterres

47

intertwined to give the same kind of effect as the pleached lime walk at Hidcote. The trunk of each apple tree is kept bare to a height of about five feet so, again as at Hidcote, the trees, although different species, appear uniform. At the base of each trunk is an upturned bowl of evergreen *Hebe rakaiensis* which looks as if it has been trimmed to make what is clearly one of John Stefanidis' favourite shapes. In fact, the hebe are not clipped; they form this shape naturally. At the far end of the path, to left and right, are two six-foot metal frames with more apple trees trained to climb up and across. The overall effect

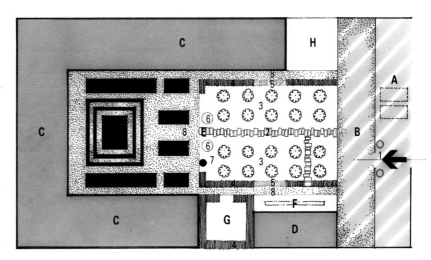

is one of symmetry and, except during blossom time, of contrasting greens. Then, with a single stroke, the whole formal symmetry is both emphasised and destroyed by a feature which bears no relation to the rest of the garden. This is to the left, at the edge of the lawn, where John Stefanidis has built a tall flint and brick pillar, about eight feet high, or rather a flint pillar with brick bracelets. On the top is a sort of sculpture of big flints which might or might not be intended to represent something. 'Saint Simon Stylites?' suggests John Stefanidis.

Beyond the orchard is the low area of box *parterre*, unusual and interesting in its detailing. It is perhaps best to go to the far end of the courtyard, as if entering the house, and then to turn round and take in the view, this time with the formal orchard furthest from you. Directly ahead is the largest *parterre*, made of two rectangles of box hedge each about a foot high, edged by wooden boarding and with a gravel 'path' between. The outer edge is a single brick frame. In the centre of this double frame of box is a rectangle of box, about five feet across, which is being allowed to grow to form a pyramid.

On either side of this central box section are two long, narrow box beds, also with brick edging

In places tables of solid box are given more interest by stepping their margins; elsewhere box hedges surround beds of cotton lavender

49

Left: *The need for constant mowing of grass round the trunks of apple trees has been avoided by growing* Hebe rakaiensis *there instead*

and filled with cotton lavender. Then, ahead of the central box section are two more box *parterres* in which the box is clipped with a ledge all round, and at the side of these two smaller box beds. In constructing this immensely successful formal courtyard, John Stefanidis was much helped by the design skills and advice of Arabella Lennox-Boyd.

All round the courtyard are planted a mixture of 'natural' shrubs and trees; these include a huge rosemary, mixed with more contrived plantings such as a much-espaliered plum, a *Magnolia grandiflora*, and a vine near two formal bays in wooden tubs. In two places the yew hedges surrounding the garden have been cut to give 'windows' into the courtyard.

This central courtyard is a very remarkable piece of garden design, unique in its effect. But on the edges of the courtyard and outside the buildings, in the garden proper, there are many other pleasing and unusual areas which, in their own way, are just as striking as the courtyard.

Rather than try to describe the garden as a whole, it is perhaps easier to pick out some of the individual spaces or small garden 'rooms'. One, to the right of the loggia, contains many of John Stefanidis' favourite plants and is a good guide to his preferences. He favours a mixture of green foliages; flowers are not excluded, but they take third place to the possibilities of shape and contrast. It is a small, square garden with a central but irregularly-shaped lawn. Surrounding it are clematis, rosemary, honeysuckle, hostas, fig and many other substantial green shrubs. John Stefanidis notes that he was much helped and influenced in his early planting by Keith Steadman. The latter, a friend of the legendary Hiram Winterbotham, has had a considerable influence on many English gardeners from his home in Gloucestershire.

The other side of the loggia is bounded by the wall of a guest cottage, and here again is a small group of favourite plants: hostas, rosemary, hardy geraniums and, beyond them, against the wall of the cottage, a judas tree which has allowed itself to be trained up the wall. 'It produces those spectacular flowers,' says John Stefanidis. Next to this is a secret garden, a small gravel area about twelve feet square. A typical Stefanidis detail is that this area is not in fact square because the corners have been 'etched' out.

The long seat at the back of this little sitting area looks at first glance as if it might be a Chatsworth chair. In fact, all the furniture is of John Stefanidis' own design, made up for him in iroko wood, based on traditional designs but with subtle differences which make each seat particularly suited to its individual location. The use of custom-built furniture is a practice John Stefanidis carries over from his interior designing. 'We often need to design a special piece for someone,' he says, 'and although it is not cheap, it may sometimes result from a need to save on costs, because if we can't afford to buy, say, a William Kent original, then we'll produce a design which works just as well and which we can afford.'

The gardens located in the large area outside the walls of the house form the boundaries of the property. One of the largest of these is an area of grass which looks across a cornfield and beyond to a wonderful view of Bradbury Ring, an iron-age fortification dating from the first century B.C. where legend has it that King Arthur received his death wound in battle and where he still returns in the form of a raven. The boundary between the garden and the cornfield is defined by a ha-ha built by Stefanidis. Costs have been saved here by using breeze blocks for the hidden retaining wall. In the grass are three large, mature chestnut trees and, at irregular intervals, three pens of rough larchwood which hold 'beds' of roses and rosemary. Roses are one of Stefanidis' enthusiasms, and the use of the pens instead of beds is a most original way of carrying through

'the spirit of the place' by echoing the original livestock paddocks.

At the far corner of this garden, furthest away from the house, is a copse. This was formerly a large area of pine trees, most of which the new owner did away with when he thinned the copse out to make his own area of woodland garden. He took the view that if this was to be a woodland garden, then garden it should be. A path wanders through the wood, the planting of which, again, is much influenced by Keith Steadman. White is the predominant colour. Beneath the trees are phlox, hydrangeas, buddleia, and an area of blue cranesbill, all growing in carefully controlled confusion. There are many examples of *Mahonia lomariifolia*, the tall one which, although tender, survives here seemingly without difficulty. At the end of the woodland walk is a small flint dove-

A pleached lime circus is being formed to act as a centre from which all the paths through the woodland garden radiate

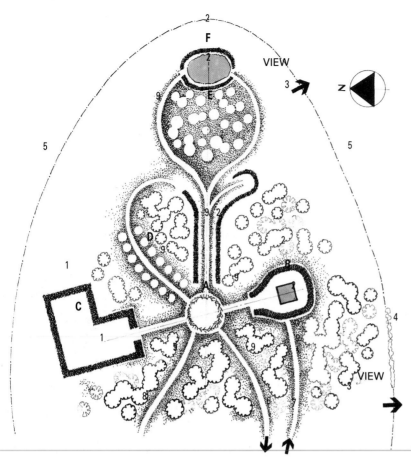

JOHN STEFANIDIS:
Woodland Garden

A Circle of 16 pleached lime trees
B Small flint dovecote in traditional pattern
C Cutting garden
D Hornbeam walk
E Russian garden: birch wood; betula jacquemontii
F Pond

1 Beech hedge
2 Box hedges
3 View points
4 Low hedge
5 Boundary fence
6 Path to main garden
7 Path from main garden
8 Dead end
9 Paths

cote, designed by John Stefanidis in a traditional pattern and erected by local builders.

To the left is another surprise, a kind of 'crossroads' at the centre of which sixteen pleached lime trees form a circle about 30 feet across. From this strong feature radiate a number of walks and entrances to yet other gardens within the garden. One of these is what John Stefanidis calls his 'Russian garden' – a small area of the birch B. jacquemontii which looks like one of those faded photographs of the garden where a Soviet writer or poet lived in a dacha exile. Another radial is a formal arched hornbeam walk. Another is a yew walk leading to a small flint-surrounded pond. A fourth area is characterised by tall obelisks of larch pole supporting old-fashioned climbing roses. Around

this are other Stefanidis favourites: day lilies and willows. Two or three dense holly trees, survivors of the original copse, have been clipped into formal shapes. Such formality underlines the fact that while this is a woodland garden, it is carefully chosen and planted. Everywhere there are surprises. A Chinese gooseberry pushes up through a holly tree. *Clematis montana* clambers up trees. And here and there are more flint columns, each differing in height or detail.

Returning to the 'crossroads', another radial takes us into a small 'cutting' garden which supplies such flowers for the house as agapanthus and old-fashioned roses. The entrance is a bridge topped by a pergola, made of elegantly detailed wood and painted a subtle reddish-purple, which John Stefanidis first spotted in an American garden near Washington. This colour 'works' with the green foliage of the wistaria which climbs along it in a way that conventional white- or green-painted wood could not. A flint path leads to the various cutting beds.

Finally, there is the water garden. The sound of water from a wall-mounted spout leads one to expect a biggish pool. What one sees instead is the *outline* of a pool, a kind of twelve-inch-wide 'frame' along which the water flows in channels cut into a surface of egg-sized cobblestones sunk in concrete. Seats at either end provide a tranquil area for calm contemplation. 'The *sound* of water is most important,' says John Stefanidis.

There is more, much more. For example, another small brick courtyard leads back to the house, with wooden benches and a huge, white canvas umbrella. To the right is a large bleached-wood conservatory within which is a small heated greenhouse, the latter used for exotica such as orchids and stephanotis.

This impression of John Stefanidis' 'cow-shed' garden began by saying that it was a place with a view. Yet each of the small gardens which make up the total cultivated area is a satisfying place to

be – they are not spaces designed simply for contemplating the view. Once outside the court-yard garden, however, beyond the boundaries of the house, there is on almost every side an opportunity to look out across a splendid English landscape of hills and forests. The designer has made every use of this view, cutting 'windows' in tree-lined borders, and keeping hedge lines low.

John Stefanidis says that he knows little enough about gardening now and knew almost nothing when he bought the place ten years ago. True, he has had the guiding hands of Keith Steadman and Arabella Lennox-Boyd but much of the design itself has been his own, such as the water-feature which was entirely his own conception. Now he is entering on a new phase as garden designer. Recently he moved into a house in London designed by Lutyens who had also created the garden there, now overgrown and rather lost beneath the weeds. Stefanidis once designed a cabinet which he named 'Tribute to Lutyens' and it will be interesting to see just what form his town garden will take as a further tribute from one designer to another.

By confining it to a rectangular channel surrounding and surrounded by beach cobbles set in cement, a small amount of water has here been used to great effect. The twinkling reflections of sunlight from the polished pebbles are reminiscent of the sparkle from a surface disturbed by wind

Michael van Valkenburgh

ON FIRM LINES

There is nothing tentative or timid in the firm, clearly expressed lines that characterise the designs of Michael Van Valkenburgh, landscape architect and associate professor of Harvard University's School of Design in Cambridge, Massachusetts, USA. He draws them clean and hard against the soft amorphousness of plants, paints striking white against deep, drab evergreens, and injects a formal, geometric solemnness into the wanton exuberance of nature. When he designs a garden, he says, he strives for simplicity and precision.

Van Valkenburgh speaks frequently about precision. Certainly his work exhibits precise attention to detail. Neat zig-zagged edgings, diamond patterns cut into steps, a careful gradation of the size of foliage plants to heighten perspective, and clearly demarked sub-spaces within a garden are typical of his work. Above all there is unstinting use of the right angle. His are gardens of great contrast.

Architectural elements in Van Valkenburgh designs are decidedly hard-edged geometry. Even the plants may be used to create formalised repetitions of the vegetation around the garden. 'I feel it's imperative to use plants with simplicity and clarity,' he states. Walls run parallel and at right angles to paths. Staircases rise in direct and regular progression from one level to another. Paths are ramrod straight and sometimes inlaid with diamonds or edged with zigzags.

Neither are paths allowed to be merely subservient to function. Instead they are ceremonial, complete unto themselves. As uncompromisingly man-made elements, they move through the natural world of the garden – a part of it and yet, curiously foreign to it. Nowhere is there the ghost of a hope that time or the growth of plants will soften their clean, hard edges.

Dazzling white arches against a backdrop of deep evergreen have been included in some of Van Valkenburgh's gardens. They are nothing if not eyecatching. They function as sculpture, a fixed focus for interest around the year. Because they are so familiar in form they are more readily acceptable than more outlandish modern sculptures but they have none of the traditional stylistic associations one attaches to urns, cherubs, and so on.

Mr Van Valkenburgh has used arches or white trellises to mark the entry from one part of the garden into another. 'I think of them as a threshold. I like to use clear markers at transition points.' His gardens are frequently divided into sub-spaces that are marked at these transition points. For instance, a pedimented arch in a garden near Boston, Massachusetts marks the transition from a perennial border to a woodland walk. This garden was divided into sub-spaces ranging in size from a small, cozy outdoor dining room to a vast lawn. The lawn, stretching between a formal rose garden and woodland, is the largest section of the garden. It has been provided with two Adirondack-style chairs of Mr Van Valkenburgh's own design. Set at a distance across the lawn, the chairs serve both to keep the garden from slipping unnoticed into the woods and as scale reference points to give a sense of its enormous sweep.

The arch, on high ground and set against feathery, deep-green hemlocks, is visible from several sections of the garden. As one moves around it, the arch appears to follow along,

Michael Van Valkenburgh designed these Adirondack-style chairs to provide a scale reference and also to mark the transition between the lawn and woodland area in a Massachusetts garden

55

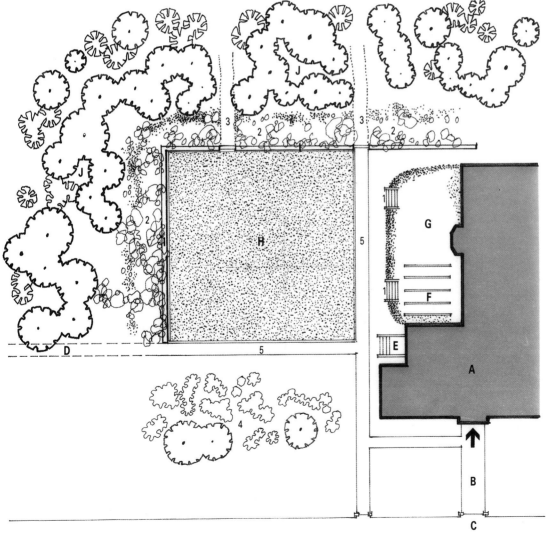

MICHAEL VAN VALKENBURGH:
Seaside Garden

A House
B Front entrance
C Roadway
D Footpath to garage
E Steps to house
F Patio
G Grassy mound
H Lawn
I Stone walls
J Woodland

1 White stone steps
2 Mixed planting: rosa rugosa; cotoneaster; sweet fern
3 Mulch paths
4 Tree and shrub planting
5 Paths

changing shape as it goes, but always a handsome and striking focus.

Dividing gardens into sub-spaces and marking the transitions are also effective techniques in small gardens, where they seem to enlarge the space available by defining and enriching experience. Arches *suggest* more to come – even when they are, in reality, at the very perimeter of a garden. Mr Van Valkenburgh has also used arches in conjunction with foreshortened paths to force perspective and fool the eye into perceiving more garden space than actually exists.

Sometimes a garden is allowed to be large and is not broken into smaller parts. Size is celebrated not in the number of parts, but in the quality of a very few strong, bold elements. This is true in a seaside garden on an island off the coast of Massachusetts. There Van Valkenburgh created a memorable space using only two fieldstone walls, two long, straight paths across lawn, and a mixed woodland's-edge planting of *Rosa rugosa*, sweet fern, and cotoneaster. 'Strong and

A white pedimented arch in a Boston-area garden marks the transition from border garden to woodland path. Dazzling against the fine, dark needles of hemlocks, this arch changes shape when viewed from different parts of the garden

simple,' is his description of the design. The two retaining walls, at right angles to each other, hold back the woods as they neatly define two sides of a great, flat rectangle of lawn. Two paths, one running along the renovated Victorian cottage and one parallel to the street complete the rectangle.

The rigidly straight flagstone paths cross each other at crisp right angles like New York City streets. The path alongside the house passes two sets of white stone steps, brilliant against the simple green of the grass. One white staircase leads to a side entrance into the house. Another climbs to an outdoor sitting area of flagstone atop a flat-topped grassy mound. The expected, a low garden of herbs or a boundary of low shrubs to set off the terrace, is not there. The flagstone terrace sits quite exposed on its flat mound. There is only grass, the same ground cover that stretches from wall to wall and between and around the paths.

'It has the kind of simplicity that summer houses near the shore have. They are pared down to absolute necessities. It is an aesthetic that can stand near the strength of the sea,' says Van Valkenburgh.

The two white staircases are carefully balanced by two stone stairways in one of the stone walls. These lead up into the woods, joining two mulch paths that disappear into the trees towards a communal tennis court. Everything is balanced: the steps, the walls, the paths. The whole forms a large rectangle. In plan, it appears the sort of satisfyingly logical and balanced design a child might make.

The experience of walking through and being in the space, however, is not that of an adult in a childish space, but the reverse. Although the stairs and paths are comfortably scaled, the great length of the paths and walls and their uncompromising rigidity suggest a ceremonial passage through a large and important place. It is an experience not unlike that of traversing one of the Mayan plazas of Guatemala or the Yucatan. Yet there are no great buildings or temples. The elements here are minimal: two long stone walls, two straight flagstone paths, a field.

The planting is equally simple. Above and all along the walls, space has been cleared of trees and given over to a mixed planting of sweet fern, *Rosa rugosa*, and cotoneaster. At first glance, they appear to be the existing vegetation at the edge of the woods. Only their uniformity along approximately 250 feet of stone wall suggests human intervention.

'The analogue for it in art is minimalism,' says Van Valkenburgh of his style, which 'tries to retain or even exacerbate the tension by a paring down of elements. Designed landscapes,' he adds, 'are often really hard to understand. It's important to have them be understood as something that came from human hands.'

The owner of the seaside property asked Van Valkenburgh to design a second garden. Unlike the first property, which was possessed of natural beauty with spacious grounds and a view of the bay, the second was not a promising project. 'We couldn't get anything to grow. It was either too moist or too dry, very steep, and very small,' says the client of his home garden. 'It's one of those problems that was taken on because he's been such a good client,' says Mr Van Valkenburgh in describing his initial reluctance in accepting the project, adding, 'and it becomes the great work!'

The space was gloomy, small, steep, and with few, if any, aesthetically pleasing elements. It was a back yard that sloped so steeply that the main floor of the house, at ground level in front, was elevated an entire storey at the back. Although small, the yard houses a garage with a driveway leading around from the side of the house. Van Valkenburgh's solution was dramatic, simple, and very satisfying. He brought in

sixteen fully-grown white-paper birch clumps, underplanted them with ferns and myrtle, and connected the first floor balcony and the lower level driveway with a straight, simple staircase. From the balcony the brilliant white birch trunks make up a very precious woodland. Where there was once only the dismal aspect of cars, the driveway, and the garage below, there is a soaring sense of being up in the trees. The flotsam and jetsam of commuter life are obscured in the gloom of this enchanted forest and for the first time in its existence, there is a reason to stand on the balcony. Now it provides a lovely and intimate lookout for observing the seasons. After the seemingly endless New England winter, it is a triumph to watch the emergence of tiny bright green leaves in spring. In summer, there is light shade and movement in the slightest breeze. In autumn the leaves turn brilliant yellow, a colour that dazzles in the sunshine and is enhanced by fog. When winter returns, the trees brighten the space with their dazzling trunks. 'A brilliant solution to an impossible problem,' is the client's half-unbelieving description of Van Valkenburgh's design.

'I'm interested,' says Michael Van Valkenburgh, 'in doing something with a simple kind of precision – a kind of leanness.'

A simple planting of 16 mature clumps of white birch with ferns and myrtle at their feet transformed an unpromising small patch of steeply sloping land into an enchanting asset offering attractions at all seasons

57

TAMING THE
WILDERNESS

Snow melts quickest on
the crests of the gently
rolling mounds which
A. E. Bye specified for
this Long Island garden.
During each thaw the
islets of exposed turf and
the linked chains of snow
in the hollows around
them make distinct and
fascinating patterns

A. E. BYE

MOOD IN THE LANDSCAPE

The designs of Connecticut landscape architect A. E. Bye are exquisite expressions of American landscape, so perfectly in harmony with their settings that they appear to have evolved naturally. It comes as no surprise, then, when Bye is sometimes compared to his predecessor Jens Jensen, who, along with his Prairie school colleagues – including Frank Lloyd Wright – found inspiration in the great prairies of the American Midwest.

> Art must come from within, and the only source from which the art of landscaping can come is our native landscape. It cannot be imported from foreign shores and be our own.
>
> Jens Jensen, *The Clearing*

Mr Bye has no preference for one type of landscape over another. He has designed rocky seaside gardens on the East Coast of the United States and rolling landscapes in the Bluegrass country of Kentucky. Neither does he bring polemics into his design philsophy. Instead, he operates with the quiet conviction that his vision of innate landscape character is correct and that to reveal the underlying mood is the only possible approach to garden design. Nevertheless, Bye's natural style can seem unacceptable to those with more conventional and narrowly defined ideas about garden design: 'looking as if nothing at all has been done' and 'deceptively simple' are terms frequently heard in conjunction with Bye's designs. But, equally, one could describe them as achieving a 'perfect fit' with their setting. Colleague Sean West Sculley, who wrote the introduction for A. E. Bye's book, *Art into Landscape, Landscape Into Art*, says that what all of Bye's designs share is an 'apparent inevitability of the solution, as if some vague expectation had been delightfully fulfilled.' Similarities of one of his works to another are to be found and understood in the revealing of an underlying approach rather than in the details of each individual garden.

Unlike many designers, Bye uses no distinctive hallmark plants, paving types, or structures. Each design is unique, undertaken in direct response to the attributes and mood of a given site, and further modified by considerations of regional landscape character and the relationship of building to site.

About twenty years ago, Bye writes, 'I became obsessed with the idea of mood in landscape.' After one of his students at Cooper Union in New York City (where Bye is an adjunct professor teaching Design and Theory of Landscape Design) showed him how moods could be captured in photographs, he began recording them in his travels throughout the United States and in

Europe, South America, and the Caribbean: 'I felt it was a great necessity to return to my students each fall with photographs of serene landscapes or humorous landscapes or mysterious landscapes,' says Bye, adding, 'everywhere upon the face of the land or sea or in the sky we can find mood.' He concedes, though, that, 'obviously mood is subjective.'

This photographic study of the landscapes of moods has made Bye a connoisseur of landscapes with profound respect and appreciation for regional characteristics. Along with native intuition, this expertise allows him to work with amazing speed. When asked by students how long it takes him to formulate a solution to a design problem, he replied, 'about two or three seconds . . . to see, in my mind's eye, an idea for a garden.' Very frequently, the inspiration for a design is one of the 'many thousands of photos illustrating different moods and visual effects.'

Observation and photographs of sand dunes in Cape Cod, Massachusetts inspired the design of the Shapiro garden, a seaside property that is, in many ways, quintessential Bye. Photos show-

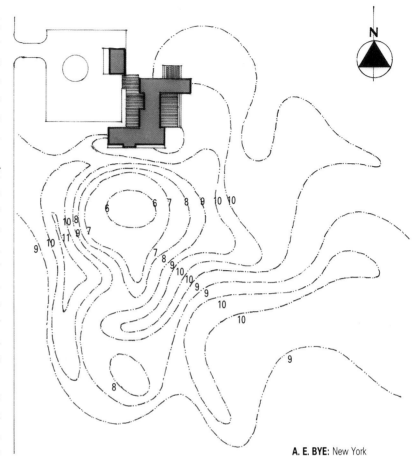

A. E. BYE: New York

61

The Shapiro residence and garden are situated on land claimed from the waters of an adjacent bay. A. E. Bye designed a garden that looks as if it evolved naturally by limiting the number of plants and involving the sky in the overall composition. Dark evergreens tie the house to the horizon line

ing the finished garden reveal a coastal landscape of great natural beauty that might easily provoke that inevitable comment: 'it looks as if nothing has been done.' In fact, when Mr Bye undertook the commission, he remembers, *everything* had to be done because the site 'was all water.' In the days before 'public hearings, permits and environmental impact statements,' the owners planned to fill eight acres with sand sucked up from the adjoining bay and to contain the newly acquired land by bulkheading. The finished site would become a peninsula 400 feet wide by 800 feet deep, projecting into the bay.

'Sand,' writes Bye in *Art into Landscape, Landscape into Art,* 'was brought in for several months until we had enough for bulldozers to create mounds and valleys. We never had to

worry about drainage,' he adds '. . . for we knew the rain would pass on through the porous sand.'

With the image of the Cape Cod dunes in mind, Bye looked to typical coastal vegetation for the planting design. 'To do this landscape,' he writes, 'it was essential to be honest with the natural hardy character of seacoast plants, the softness of sand dunes and the sensuousness of dune grasses. The landscape was to billow up and down, with voids and solids, but unified and made coherent by the all-pervading grass.'

Recalling the southern plantations along the James River in Virginia in which only lawn, oaks and English box created 'superb romantic landscapes of great sensitivity and power,' Bye knew that the number of different kinds of plants could be quite severely limited to produce a strong

In the rolling bluegrass country of Kentucky, A. E. Bye designed a 450-foot ha-ha to replace a visually disturbing horse fence. The native stone wall fits so well into the curves of the land that it has an organic quality

design. On the entire eight acres, only five kinds of plants were used; 'It's just enough,' he states. To the five types of plants: 'bayberry, pine, grass, juniper, and "free spun" yew,' a sixth design element was added: 'the sky.' Finally, the work needed time to mellow.

'Two years after the filling was complete, we brought in several thousand bayberry and a few hundred Japanese black pine and disposed them sinuously in undulating masses over and around the domed sand dunes . . . Then a wait for a few years for our work to mellow and grow to proper scale,' he writes. Time and natural processes gracefully completed the picture. Dune grasses grew from seed 'already in the sand' and 'as time went by the pines and bayberry seeded, further naturalizing our first determinations.'

In the finished, mellowed work, great expanses of shimmering grasses counterbalance the sky, while the deep green of pine, juniper, and yew anchors the house to the horizon line. It is a landscape of great contrasts, of 'voids and solids.' 'Each [of the elements] much plays against the others': the bayberries are dense and of the deepest green; they contrast in form, weight and colour with blowing, moving, shining grasses. 'The sharp and assertive pine' is in contrast with the 'benign edge of dunes,' as are all of the natural elements with the man-made straight lines of the house.

While there is great contrast and movement and changing seasonal colours, the Shapiro garden also enjoys the sense of permanence one associates with great landforms such as cliffs or mountains. This timelessness is a quality frequently found in Bye's designs. The fact that there are no forced foci or axes superimposed upon the land allows the viewer to consider the design as an entity, elevating the whole. It becomes not something small and pieced and contrived, but something of permanence and grandeur – something timeless.

Perhaps nowhere is Bye's grand simplicity so perceptible as on the Gaines estate in the Bluegrass country of Kentucky. Here, to replace a visually disturbing horse-fence, Mr Bye constructed a stone ha-ha 450 feet long – a serpentine form that was 'profiled to echo the clean rises and falls of the surrounding fields . . . and the edge of a lake across the valley.' 'When horizontal echoes vertical,' states Bye, 'there is a wonderful knitting together of what you are doing with what is happening in the distance.' Like a well tailored seam, the wall runs between levels that 'become thinner and fatter – the profile expands and contracts and creates tension between the lines.' The wall moves across the land with a graceful rhythm that unifies and plays against the adjacent elements of landscape: trees, shadows, rolling land, and distant tree line. The finished wall has an organic quality; its stone curves, echoing both the horizontal and the vertical, fit so well into those of the land that it looks as though it somehow *grew* into place. Perfect fit and the use of fitting material – native stone that is layered in the manner of many other miles of wall in the vicinity – augment the sense of permanence. To achieve this harmony, Bye used 'an instinctive approach'. He spent weeks moving the soil around so that the wall would disappear when viewed from above and create varied profiles and 'tension lines and spaces' when viewed from below.

Moving around the earth on the Gaines estate made it possible to fit a wall into the landscape. In yet another garden, the Soros garden, Mr Bye has bulldozed soil into a kind of landscape sculpture. Describing the Soros property as one designed for people living in a 'man-made town in a man-made landscape,' Mr Bye concludes, 'it follows that it be wholly man-made.' Man-made it was. For six weeks, under the direction of staff landscape architect Peter Johnson, a bulldozer and grader pushed around four acres of soil. The

63

When designing his long wall, A. E. Bye knew that its sinuous line would be just as appropriate and intriguing a feature in a rural landscape as an uncluttered highway or railway track – something associated with but unspoilt by human activity

client had seen and admired an 'open rolling landscape' in England. Eventually the desired effect was achieved when 'profiles slowly emerged as soft and sequential lines.'

The gentle hills, ridges and valleys are covered with lawn and studded here and there – on the crest of hills or in depressions – with what Bye describes as 'grouplings' of bayberry. Both the hills and the groups of bayberry confuse one's comprehension of space and 'appear larger than they really are because there is no human arte-fact nearby to give correct scale.' The result is that the lawn creates an illusion of vastness. No one hill or tree or valley stands out as a focus, so that the whole surface occupies the centre of interest and this, too, enlarges rather than dimi-nishes the space.

Here again, the number of plants used has been severely limited. There are only three: Japanese black pine, bayberry, and grass. In this way, states Mr Bye, one can better 'enjoy the nuances of the contouring – how the shadow rolls up and down the hills.' Hills and valleys give a gently undulating, moving surface to the land that is like the roll of the sea. For most of the year, subtle gradations of colour and shadow play over the surface, changing as the day pro-gresses. In winter, however, dramatic patterns emerge and become pronounced as the snow melts unevenly over the rolling surface.

All along the edges is a dark rim of both evergreen and deciduous trees against which the gentle hills are seen in profile. In early morning and late afternoon, the trees cast long shadows over the lawn. Like zebra stripes, they radiate out over mounds and ridges and become splayed and distorted by uneven ground forms.

In all of these gardens Bye has kept the number of design elements to a minimum. Some-times, as in the Shapiro and Soros gardens, the few elements are repeated many times over. Repetition enables existing features of the most

subtle nature – shadows or nuances of colour – to play a prominent role. The mood or 'person-ality' of the landscape is also strengthened by the controlled repetition of a few carefully selected elements.

Bye does more than simply limit design ele-ments such as the kinds and numbers of trees and plants; he has also been known to *subtract* from a landscape, by thinning trees, exposing rock, or extending a clearing. By omitting what is ex-traneous, he abstracts each landscape to its essence. Of a garden on which he is currently working on Long Island in New York, he de-scribes his method: seeing 'crooked trees' grow-ing in a group amongst straight ones, he says, 'I will chop down these nice trees so the crooked ones are left.'

By correctly ascertaining the mood of a par-ticular landscape and then doing whatever is necessary – subtracting, adding, or multiplying parts of the design, he draws out the innate character of the garden. Whatever is done, however, always follows as a logical consequence of the existing conditions of the site. 'I see it and then I enhance it,' says A. E. Bye of the latent mood of a site. 'I don't need to go fooling around with a whole bunch of studies and drawings. You see what to do at the very beginning. There's not much use in trying another idea.'

A. E. Bye has always been a man ahead of his time. To buck the tide, he reflects, 'you have to have a lot of conviction and be courageous. You have to persevere with this thing . . . and send out the same signals . . . for decades before it sinks into our society.' Without apology, he de-scribes his philosophy as 'all platitudes,' but sticks to it. The reward for this tenacity is in the designs he creates. 'If you create a certain quality of mood, that will be meaningful to people in the future. If it is done with great vigour and convic-tion, with meaning and integrity, then it becomes a timeless thing.'

GILLES CLEMENT

THE TAME IN THE WILD

According to the French landscaper Gilles Clement, no garden should be considered to possess style unless it can be clearly identified as an expression of the personality of its creator. 'Otherwise,' he says, 'it would simply be a piece of decor.' This is, he thinks, why public gardens, since they offer so few opportunities for personal expression, seldom manifest style and are merely green spaces between buildings.

'In what public gardens can one find anything approaching the wonderfully stylish alliance of formal architectural features and diverse plant material which exists in Vita Sackville-West's garden at Sissinghurst in Kent? That resulted from the individual vision of a gifted designer.'

Other English gardens where he is conscious of a strong sense of style are Hidcote Manor and Kiftsgate Court in Gloucestershire whose Mediterranean equivalents he thinks might be the Jardins Noailles at Grasse or the Chèvre d'Or at Biot, both in the *Alpes Maritimes* or, in quite a different idiom, the wonderful Moorish garden of the Generalife at the Alhambra in Granada.

A great plantsman at heart, Clement has done many stylish things with plants in the fifty-plus gardens which he has created. He has a great gift for unusual colour effects, the result of the careful association of plants. In the deep blue shade beneath trees in a Normandy garden, he located

Pieris 'Forest Flame', *Rhododendron luteum*, *R.* '*Koeningin Emma*', and *R.* '*Persil*' to produce a flare of orange over a ground-cover of *Tellima grandiflora* – chosen because it has 'a fragrance resembling that of azaleas'; an observation which prompts the notion that style need not be confined to the visual. The happy juxtaposition of fragrances or the contrivance of particular arrangements of plants, masonry or such features as windflutes, while hinting at gimmickry, may, when employed by genuine stylists, help to impart a unique stamp on a garden.

Planting massed red cabbages between blocks of orange potentilla achieved a notably stylish effect in an area of a garden which Clement created in the Creuse. As well as striving for strikingly unusual colour contrasts or harmonies by means of plant association, he also obtains wonderful effects by confronting the bold forms of shrubs such as yew or hornbeam – clipped into balls, ovals or cubes – with tall slender plants such as miscanthus or irises, phormiums and day lilies. He has also been very successful in imposing one plant form upon another as, for example, when allowing the clematis 'Hagley Hybrid' to clamber through *Rosa sinensis mutabilis* or *Senecio greyi*. That is a game which Gertrude Jekyll also enjoyed playing.

Clement's most interesting accomplishments have not been restricted to his work with plants:

Planted and tended initially, clumps of lupins self-seed and luxuriate at the foot of trees in Gilles Clement's garden

Below: *Proud tails of Eremurus enjoy their moment of glory among the jostle of plants near the house*

GILLES CLEMENT: Garden Plan

A House
B Oak glades
C Courtyard
D Beechwood
E Stream
F Broader pools

1 Wildflower meadow
2 Rough grass lawn
3 Climbers like Fremontodendron californicum, Actinidia chinensis, Clematis orientalis and Vitis coignetiae on the house wall
4 Feature shrubs including Acer japonicum 'Aureum', Abelia X grandiflora, Rhododendron yakusimanum and Nandinia domestica
5 Euphorbias, Ceanothus, Lavandula, Senecio, Thymus, Hebe and Geranium
6 Pink flowered plants including Cornus kousa, Rosa 'Alberic Barbier', Rosa chinensis 'Mutabilis' and Camellia sasanqua 'Maiden's Blush'
7 Shrubbery: Pieris, Hamamelis and Garrya
8 Trees and shrubs: Robinia pseudoacacia 'Frisia', Skimmia japonica and Polygonatum multiflorum
9 Rocky area: Cistus, Olearia, Yuccas and Abutilons
10 Perennials: Alliums and Hellebores
11 The orange garden: Azaleas, Mimulus, Viburnum farreri and Photinias

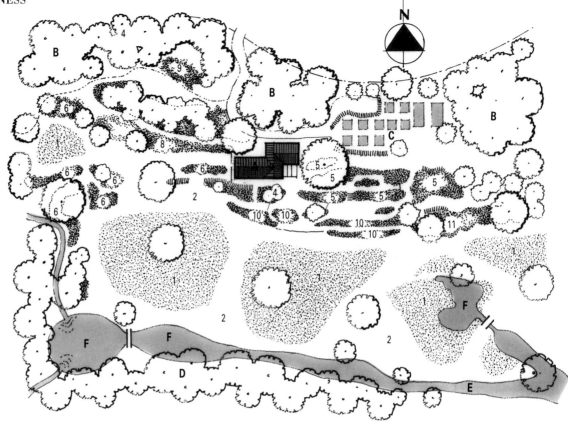

in one of his projects he replaced a central, vertical fountain jet in a rectangular pond with a laterally-mounted circular cluster of narrow horizontal jets, creating an exciting new water-garden feature.

But the arrangement of hard artefacts has always been of less concern to Gilles Clement than the selective use of plants. In his own garden, on several acres of a shallow wooded valley in the Creuse *département* near Limoges, he has created one of the most stylish 'natural' gardens in France. This land, which Clement acquired in 1978, has provided the raw material for his research into the transformation of land which has formerly carried crops or tended meadows and then for many years been abandoned to the whims of nature. By very careful and selective removal of the indigenous plants which have reinvaded the area – sometimes pruning trees and shrubs which he left and then introducing

thoughtfully chosen exotics – he has achieved remarkable results. After ten years, he has created an atmosphere of a world apart – of somewhere not quite tamed. In spirit it has a lot in common with the charming jungly paintings of the impressionist Douanier Rousseau. What's more, it requires very little maintenance.

'Gardening in this way demands a certain attitude,' Clement explained. 'It is necessary to accept the dynamism of vegetation with serenity. One must not be upset by superabundance, but be able to accept joyously the apparent anarchy of rampaging plants, recognising their richness and diversity.'

In order to adopt this approach successfully, it is vital to understand what particular plants can offer. 'You have to remember what plants look like and what they will become; when, where and how they will flower or lose foliage and die back; how they will survive in the face of unbridled competition for air, soil, water, nutrients and light. Without this knowledge, there will always be a tendency to be over-solicitous about the plants, to circumscribe and try to master the most vigorous. And the life and vigour of the plants must be privileged to the detriment of form and order. Otherwise the magic sense of freedom is lost.'

Clement recognises that an untamed wilderness can be forbidding and that the variety of vegetation offered by a particular area is often very restricted. Just accepting such a situation might be good conservation, 'but it isn't gardening.' He subscribes to the view that landscapes are always more interesting and reassuring when they are unmistakably modelled by the activities of man.

The first task in his own garden was to enrich the indigenous vegetation by establishing trees, shrubs, herbaceous plants and hundreds of bulbs. With the exception of the bulbs, the ground was cleared for planting and weeded for a foot or two round the plant bases for a couple of seasons to allow the newcomers a real chance to become firmly established before they were left to survive on their own.

To introduce the notion of husbandry – the idea that someone is caring for and modelling the land – and to assist access to most areas, Clement mows grass alleys through his wilderness, sometimes bridging them with planted arches. Leaving many of the common hornbeams and other trees and shrubs which he found on the land in their natural state, he has gently clipped others into spheres or columns.

'I have tried to produce a garden which is constantly changing. There is always something rather static about the truly "wild garden" of Bacon, since a balance has long been established, whereas my garden changes almost beyond recognition every year. This would be a little uncomfortable if I hadn't used rather obvious clipped forms and taken great care to provide constant reassuring reference points from which the plant pageant can be observed.'

At La Berthonnière, Clement's visitors have a season-long pageant to admire. Among the several areas of wildflower meadow (which are only topped once a year) feature shrubs such as golden acers, *Abelia* X *grandiflora*, *Rhododendron yakusimanum* and *Nandinia domestica* which add interest above ground level. In the drier, sunny areas, a glorious jumble of euphorbia, ceanothus, lavandula, senecio, thymus, hebe and geranium flourishes, often in competition with their wild cousins.

Yucca gloriosa, *Abutilon vitifolium* (allowed to mountaineer unaided), cistus of several types and olearia all bestow a colourful cladding of foliage and flowers on rockier land. Hornbeams 'socked' in ivy rise out of a jungle of rheum, lungwort, lupin and tussocky grass at their feet. High, acid-yellow plumes of eremurus hold their own against boisterous ragwort in a deep pasture sward.

In marrying the tame with the wild in this way, Clement has created a landscape of his own which is every bit as stylish as those portrayed in the paintings of Rousseau.

69

Although much of the cleared area of the garden is dedicated to flower meadow which is only mown twice a year, it is penetrated by closely mown paths indicating the presence of man the gardener

*Gilles Clement always
encourages his
herbaceous plants to
develop into large,
meaningful clumps
which are not dominated
by the heavy leafiness of
the woodlands around*

Wolfgang Oehme and James van Sweden

ORNAMENTAL GRASSES

When landscape architect James van Sweden of Oehme, van Sweden & Associates spoke at Harvard University in the autumn of 1986, there was standing room only. Students, landscape architects, nurserymen, and gardeners had crowded in to hear about and see examples of a new style of landscaping that is transforming gardens on the East Coast of the United States.

Gradually, this 'new American garden', characterised by soft, flowing ground cover of herbaceous plants and ornamental grasses, is making inroads in other parts of the country. All along the interstate highways that traverse the expansive states of the American Midwest, isolated examples of the new style are appearing in the larger cities and university towns. Suddenly there are ornamental grasses and fields of perennials where ivy and boxwoods used to be. Virtually singlehandedly, the firm of Oehme, van Sweden & Associates is changing the palette of plants used in American garden design.

The 'Oehme' of Oehme, van Sweden is Wolfgang Oehme, president of the firm, horticulturist and landscape architect. For Mr Oehme, the new American garden is not so much new as an American offshoot of a style that was developing in Germany before World War II. In the Thirties, Karl Foerster, a remarkable nurseryman and horticultural writer from Bornim, championed the use of ornamental grasses in the garden, spoke about 'wild garden design', and fought for the establishment of public demonstration and trial gardens. Oehme, who was educated in Berlin, visited just such a public garden in Hamburg – *Planten und Blomen* – for the first time in 1952. He was to return every year throughout the Fifties. The varieties of ornamental grasses and perennials and the way in which they were planted made a deep impression on him. When he arrived in America in 1958, ready to put his new ideas to work, however, he found he was a voice 'crying in the wilderness.'

In America Oehme found a clearcut separation between landscaping and gardening: 'landscaping' meant lawns, evergreen ground cover and shrubbery; 'gardening' included everything else and was generally done in the back yard next to the garage. Landscape architects filled their plans with lawns, evergreen ground covers, and shrubs. Herbaceous plants were never considered part of a design. Once in a while a plan would set aside a little garden space with the notation 'flowerbed to be planted by owner'. Americans had come to expect nice, neat landscaping that was evergreen.

'I had to convince people' to use herbaceous material, Mr Oehme explains. Once he had overcome that stumbling block, there was another one: 'There were no plants available – no perennials – no grasses period!' After setting up his own practice he looked in vain for a nursery that carried ornamental grasses. Finally, for his first commission at Goucher College, he says, 'I just dug them up in the field – some naturalised *Miscanthus.*'

Thirty years later, Oehme's firm is famous for its use of ornamental grasses and perennials. It is largely thanks to the company's influence that plants once unknown in America such as *Perovskia atriplicifolia, Miscanthus purpurescens,* or *Ligularia dentata* are becoming readily available. Among the dozens of species of grasses and perennials the firm uses, two plants have become hallmarks: black-eyed Susan (*Rudbeckia fulgida* 'Goldsturm') and fountain grass (*Pennisetum alopecuroides*).

'Peculiar to America . . . is a nostalgia for open land, the frontier, if you will, which is recalled in the inclusion of ornamental grasses – originally bred by Karl Foerster. It took Wolfgang, an immigrant from Germany, to recognise the natural beauty of ornamental grasses as a metaphor for the American meadow,' explains van Sweden.

Another reason for the enormous popularity of this style is the fact that it requires relatively low maintenance. In the United States, only a devoted gardener will find the time and have the knowledge to maintain any but the least demanding of plants. Households in which all adult members are employed outside the home are becoming the rule. Most people want to come home and *relax* in the garden, not spend the weekend doing garden chores. 'In America, where skilled landscape help is expensive and difficult to find, one solves maintenance problems ahead of time by judicious choice and placement of plants,' states Mr van Sweden. Those chosen are the kind Karl Foerster described as '*Ordnungshelden*', for which the American equivalent might be 'plants with the right stuff'.

These are plants a cut above all the rest: trouble-free, outstanding individuals that always look good, that succeed without mollycoddling, the heroes of their class. If they are perennials, they are vigorous, but not invasive. They do not need staking, cutting back, or frequent division. Above all, they are presentable for the longest possible period. Among them are *Rudbeckia fulgida* 'Goldsturm,' *Sedum telephium* 'Autumn Joy', astilbes, *Coreopsis verticillata*, and many ornamental grasses. And the select few plants chosen are used in large quantity.

In Oehme, van Sweden gardens, then, herbaceous perennials and ornamental grasses are used in great masses. Installing large groups of a single type of plant simplifies maintenance, something that is important in large corporate or public gardens. Even the least skilled help can be instructed to 'pull out everything that doesn't look like this or this.' Massing also has enormous visual impact. It takes the effect of a single plant and enlarges its scale to one that is truly noticeable in the landscape. When large blocks of a perennial are planted together, all the dynamics of a single plant's growth – emergence, bloom,

73

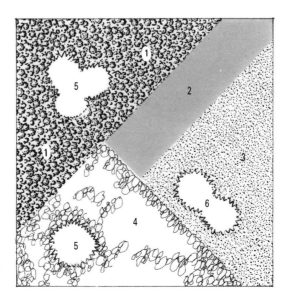

FEDERAL RESERVE GARDEN, WASHINGTON DC designed by Oehme, Van Sweden and Associates

1 Field of epimedium
2 Field of calamagrosis
3 Field of liriope spicata
4 Field of bergenia
5 Miscanthus sinensis 'Gracillimus'
6 Miscanthus sinensis

Masses of black-eyed Susans, Rudbeckia fulgida *'Goldsturm' and ornamental grasses create a formal meadow at the Federal Reserve Garden in Washington DC*

slowly changing colour – are magnified into a landscape feature. Thus, something that is easily overlooked in a landscape, because by itself it is small and fleeting, becomes an eye-stopping spectacle. Even a small plant from the perennial border can make a dramatic seasonal statement when used in masses that, as James van Sweden says, 'can be read at thirty miles per hour.'

All phases of a plant's development contribute to the overall design. One's delight in the chance discoveries of the spring garden: the unfurling of a fern, the sudden appearance of blunt bullet-heads of hosta, or the red lacy leaves of young astilbes, are here multiplied by hundreds into a striking image that defines the season. A hundred emerging grasses racing with the foliage of daffodils and tulips is a dynamic portrayal of the breathless, headlong rush of spring growth. Summer's buxom maturity is powerfully ex-

pressed in lush meadows of rudbeckia and fountain grass. A field of dove-coloured achillea seed-heads left on apple-green plants conveys the sense of lingering departure, the reluctant withering, that is autumn. Winter's period of waiting is watched over by stiffly erect ornamental grasses, struck brittle and almond-coloured by frost.

Massed garden subjects at the International Center garden in Washington, DC – an Oehme, van Sweden design – turn an entire landscape into garden. Instead of a single Sedum 'Autumn Joy' emerging in April, forming flat flower umbels in July, turning pink in September, and copper-coloured in October, an entire hillside does so.

There is always something new and different to see. Elsewhere in the International Center's garden, a field of *Coreopsis verticillata* 'Moon-

In late autumn,
deep-rose-coloured
flowers of 'Autumn Joy'
sedums contrast with
dried Miscanthus
purpurescens *and the*
deep green of Nelly
Stevens holly in the
Federal Reserve Garden

75

shine' blooms lemon yellow in summer. After blooming, it stays bright green spotted with dark brown seed pods for another month or two, then turns into clouds of frost-darkened foliage. In winter, this smoky brown contrasts smartly with the pale winter tones of dried ornamental grasses.

Before being redesigned by Oehme and van Sweden, the Federal Reserve Bank Building in Washington had typical American institutional landscaping: lawn, boxwoods, and azaleas. Now, flowing masses of herbaceous plants – 'Autumn Joy' sedums, 'Goldsturm' rudbeckias, fountain grass, *Miscanthus purpurescens*, and 'Ruby Glow' sedums – combine in dynamic tapestries.

In a large square planter that is located over an underground parking garage, Oehme and van Sweden have installed a sophisticated meadow of interlocking wedges of epimediums, bergenias, creeping lily turf, and the ornamental grass, *Calamagrostis*. Large maiden grasses (*Miscanthus sinensis* 'Gracillimus') and Eulalia grass (*M. sinensis*) provide strong, vertical accents.

A wild-looking garden in the city is refreshing. In an isolated suburban setting, it is spectacular. The windblown, natural appearance of a seaside meadow was exactly what Carole and Alex Rosenberg wanted for their private garden on New York's Long Island when they hired Oehme, van Sweden & Associates. Located on a little inlet, the property is fringed with native reeds along the water's edge. Leading into these is a broad, low planting of masses of fountain grass, blue oat grass, lavender, *Perovskia*, and *Achillea* punctuated by tall maiden grass (*Miscanthus sinensis* 'Gracillimus'), moor grass (*Molinia* 'Windspiel'), and porcupine grass (*M. sinensis zebrinus strictus*). This stylised meadow provides a perfect transition to the surrounding natural vegetation.

Low plantings also create a sense of enclosure in two outdoor living areas without obscuring a splendid view of the water. French doors from a spacious living room and two bedrooms open onto an outdoor dining terrace that is edged by a low hedge of fountain grass, *Pennisetum alopecuroides*, and Eulalia grass, *Miscanthus sinensis*. Seated at the dining table on this dark flagstone terrace, one enjoys an unimpaired view of the inlet and its abundant bird life.

From the terrace a flagstone path leads around to the side of the house where a vegetable and cutting garden provides summer flowers, lettuce, tomatoes, and herbs. Leading in the other direction, another path passes a mass planting of lavender, *Perovskia*, and a sweet bay magnolia, *M. virginiana*, and ends up on a lower terrace around an oval, black-bottomed swimming pool. When the water is still, large summer mounds of maiden grass and red, summer-blooming hibiscus are reflected on the surface.

Between pool and inlet is a staggered planting of day lilies, lythrum, *Miscanthus purpurescens*, *Miscanthus sinensis* and, finally, the native reed, *Phragmites*. In summer, this part of the garden is lush with the dense foliage of grasses and herbaceous plants. There is constant movement as breezes from the inlet sweep across the grasses. Deep within the planting, dozens of birds take shelter.

In spring, hundreds of bulbs provide two months of bright colour. Daffodils are followed by tulips; these, in turn, dovetail with the return of the ornamental grasses with which they have been interplanted. By the time the tulips are spent, the grasses are tall enough to act as camouflage. In summer, the grasses come to perfection. Voluminous matt-green mounds neutralise potentially clashing colours while their heights and habits relieve the monotony of uniform masses of lavender, achillea, lythrum, and day lilies. Moving in the slightest breeze, they bring sound into the garden too. Their

Ornamental grasses and masses of perennials lend a wild, natural look to the Rosenbergs' waterside garden on Long Island

77

seemingly wild, blowing forms are perfectly suited to the seaside setting.

Ornamental grasses also have the advantage of being late bloomers. Silken flower tassels and feathery seedheads appear in the autumn when little else is flowering. In a planted island in the driveway in front of the Rosenberg house, *Miscanthus purpurescens*, a medium-sized grass that stays quietly green all summer, glows bright red in the autumn sunshine. It is, however, for their winter appearance that grasses are best known and loved. In the Rosenberg garden the winter forms and colours of *Miscanthus sinensis* 'Gracillimus' and *M.s. zebrinus strictus* and the native *Phragmites* are especially effective. And with the loss of their summer volume, the view of the water becomes more prominent. 'Anyone,' states James van Sweden, 'can do a spring garden. That is easy because most ornamental plants bloom at this time. To create a garden with interest for *all* seasons requires a large number of different plants.' In the Rosenberg garden, the large number of plants that contribute colour and beauty in spring, summer, and autumn, contribute handsomely to the winter garden as well. A skilful combination of perennials and grasses are woven into a cover of subdued winter colours. Masses of smaller grasses like fountain or switch grass glow in the sombre winter landscape like fields of golden wheat. Seedheads left on perennial plants, leafless trees, a sparing use of evergreens, and bright almond-coloured giant grasses make up a rich winter tapestry of subtle and naturally harmonious colours perfectly adjusted to winter's muted light.

Jim van Sweden describes his firm's practice of designing natural processes into gardens as 'mediating between man and nature', or 'managing the middle'. Before installation, plants are painstakingly chosen for colour, height, and length of show. Then they are carefully situated in the landscape. Once in place, however, they are allowed to grow into natural shapes. The result is a design that is both formal and uniform enough for a public space, but at the same time as spontaneous as a meadow. Wolfgang Oehme says, 'our job is to provide the framework . . . and let the plants express themselves.'

Delight in the rhythmic changing of the earth's flora is as old as gardening itself. In the designs of Oehme, van Sweden it has become a dynamic, new style: a new American garden.

Ramona Sahm

GRASS AND LEAVES

In Ramona Sahm's large, enclosed courtyard, the fig trees have been undersown with thousands of annual nasturtiums. It's the sort of cheeky and inexpensive grand gesture which anyone could afford but which only a truly stylish gardener would have the nerve to make

Not far from San Diego and perhaps an hour's drive from the Mexican border, Ramona Sahm has planted an entire hilltop with uncommon vision. Hers is a garden of simplicity and great luxury. For throughout the long, rainless California summer, when vegetation on the surrounding hills withers to buff and tan, Ramona's simple garden of grass glows a rich emerald green. Her hilltop acres are provided with a constant supply of what in this landscape is the most precious commodity of all: water.

Irrigation keeps this hilltop garden green and luxuriant. Ramona delights in and shows ap-

preciation for a profusion of verdant grass by allowing it to grow lush and long. When it is cut it is not done so in the even, slightly overlapping strips that make for a closely trimmed, velvety lawn. Instead, Ramona does the mowing herself – wherever and whenever the spirit moves her. The resulting patterns of long, medium, and short grass compose a kind of living green paisley jacquard that spills down the hill behind her house until it meets the dry valley below.

Green is the dominant colour in this garden although there are clumps, here and there, of day lilies, New Zealand impatiens, and bougainvillea. These provide tantalising spots of colour in an immense sea of greens. Different lengths of grass exhibit different shades. When the wind blows, swathes of long grass change colours, turning briefly silver in the sunlight and smokey blue in shadow.

Because the hilltop is high above the clamour of the valley below, there is profound calm in this garden. Voices fall away. The shushing of wind in the tall grass and the rustling of leaves in the trees are the only sounds of consequence.

Trees are the garden's other luxury. For Ramona, the greatest treasure of all is a gnarled mesquite (*Prosopis*) that was transplanted fully grown to its hilltop site. 'We are not young enough to start with a young tree,' Ramona says of her beloved mesquite. 'We transplanted large

trees so that we could enjoy them right away.' The mesquite looks as though it has stood in place for at least a half century. For Ramona, its grassy shade is a favoured spot for reflection.

Elsewhere, groups of the California plane tree (*Platanus californica*) have been planted. Their light-coloured, exfoliating bark contrasts with the dark of the house and the low green of the grass landscape. Seemingly random groves of California plane trees lend a wonderfully natural feeling to the back garden.

In contrast, an entrance garden on the front side of the house is carefully controlled. In an enclosed courtyard, about 70 feet in length, very large fig trees are rhythmically spaced and underplanted with a ground cover of nasturtium.

Scraps of orange and red and yellow flowers poke out from under the round leaves, shy accents to a mass of green texture. A Japanese-style covered verandah runs along the house side of the courtyard whilst fieldstone walls enclose the other sides.

Ramona's courtyard and the grassy meadow behind the house are gardens that know no prototypes. They have grown out of their owner's singular preferences for the lushness of grass, the sparing use of colour in an expanse of green, and the repetition of a very few kinds of plants in a garden of grand proportions. 'Doing one's own thing,' a California precept, has seldom been carried out in a garden with such elegance or simplicity.

Long, lush grass is an expensive luxury on a Southern Californian hilltop in summer because it can only be maintained by constant irrigation. However, what may be commonplace elsewhere here becomes exceptional due to its rarity

79

NEW ROMANTICS

There are few more romantic sights than an archway of old roses

Joyce Robinson and John Brookes

STREAMS AND PASTURES NEW

A moody discontent with the mundane fostered Joyce Robinson's development into one of Britain's most stylish gardeners. 'I did not want flowers,' says Mrs Robinson, who began the planting of Denmans in 1947. 'It was form and colour from plants that made up the structure of my garden.'

Her garden was formerly the kitchen garden and stableyard of Westergate House, the home of the then Lord Denman, in a sheltered setting at the foot of the South Downs in West Sussex. This is how Joyce Robinson describes the garden she created: 'One can never recover that first, fine, careless rapture when planning or planting a new site. For the next year – perhaps two – while thinking what we would do with it, we grew anything that would sell – self-blanching celery, Dutch iris, early strawberries. By 1950 I decided such hard work was getting too much for us so we gave up the market-garden crops altogether and grew some wonderful vegetables. We laid out a conventional vegetable garden, peas and beans properly staked, parsley and herb edges, the lot! Much more than we could eat but not enough to market. Herbs seemed to be the answer, so in about a third of the garden I planted both culinary and medicinal herbs, also many herb-like plants to give height and substance. These I planted in well-prepared soil, then covered the lot with water-worn gravel. I had not the time to look after a traditionally-patterned herb garden, so everything that I thought went with herbs had a place, and was encouraged to seed. Thus by pulling up the unwanted plants, be they weed or herbs, a picture was built up that gave a long flowering season and all the herbs we needed in the kitchen.

'I still had the greater part of the garden and the walls to plant. I was thinking of a profusion of growing beauty: beauty of shape and winter colour, the walls festooned with roses and clematis. In these irregular groups of colour beset with winding paths I planted a few small trees, thus making some shade. I chose a free-standing apricot for its shape and beauty of spring foliage, and an arbutus for its pink trunk and its interesting flowers and fruit that are produced together in the autumn. A very silver-leaved eucalyptus, un-named, and a *Robinia pseudoacacia frisia* are planted so closely that they grow through each other.

'This walled garden faces nearly due south and has three openings, on the north, south and west. In hot weather, it gets very dry, and strong winds tend to flow around the walls and damage the climbers, but mostly it is very quiet and still, with a remote, enclosed feeling, and as it is closely planted and overflowing it seems bigger than it actually is. In high summer it can be the enchanted garden of one's childhood.

'And the walls? Being planted both sides, many things give colour and interest by just peeping over. The wistaria touches the ground on both sides and *Clematis orientalis* grows up, over and into everything. *Magnolia grandiflora*, untrained, makes a good patch of dark evergreen well above the top of the wall, and is host to Campsis (Madame Galen) on one side and *Vitis coignetiae* on the other. A careful cut-back to keep their shape in the autumn, and a top dressing of cow manure at least every three years and they will go on in good health for ever. I use no artificial manure, not even for the roses.'

After 20 years of gardening, Joyce Robinson began to feel the first pangs of dissatisfaction. She became bored with grass and soil and searched in her mind for a third medium. Should it be water? Or should it be rock?

In 1969 Joyce Robinson went to Greece and the Greek Islands and found there her inspiration for the changes she was to make. Her search for another texture, another medium, ended at Delos, an island covered with flowers. Plants and climbers grew in the land to which they belonged, cascading over and through ancient urns and pillars, tumbling down deep open wells and water holes, covering steps and the stairs. Everything grew in hot, dry, gravelly

Herbs can be confined to particular areas by planting them in gaps deliberately left in paving for that purpose. The effect is more charming if, as here at Denmans, the paving gaps are asymmetrically arranged

83

84

At Denmans it is almost impossible to see the walls in summer because they are so festooned with plants which are allowed to spill and seed with abandon

and labour-saving. Of course, weeds will grow but the annual ones are easier to pull out, and one would not start a gravel area if infested with perennial weeds. As I have no straight edges to my plantings, I can vary the shapes of the groups of colour, and the pattern of flowers or leaves, by running the gravel into the plants or popping a few further out into the gravel.

'Quite large areas of gravel sparsely planted, with a background of small trees with interesting bark, can make a quiet place to put a seat. *Acer* 'Senkaki' has bright pink stems all the winter and the leaves colour well; *Euonymus planipes* and *alatus* would make a satisfying October picture. Be careful not to clutter such a space; a few plants chosen to give interest round the year are sufficient.

'Bulbs, of course, for all seasons, starting with snowdrops and crocus, then scillas and *Chionodoxa luciliae*, which seed themselves everywhere without fail. Daffodils and tulips, early and late, of all descriptions, in large clumps of one colour, to fit in with an evergreen design. *Gladiolus byzantinus*, alliums, *Amaryllis bella-donna*, *Galtonia candicans*, kaffir lily (*Schizo-stylis*), sternbergias, fritillarias and many more. Small blue hyacinths under trees make a good picture. I plant the taller growing bulbs such as *Crinum powellii*, preferably the white one, liliums, some alliums and the wild Greek gladioli that seed themselves everywhere and can be a nuisance, among shrubs or under a wall. We seldom stake anything: my aim is to plant closely, next to something that will not only give support, but will complement its neighbour. The garden is supposed to depict glorious disarray – I some-times wonder if glorious is the right word.'

Having brought gravel gardening to Denmans, Joyce Robinson then took to another challenge – a small paddock left within the walled area. The idea came to her quite suddenly: why not gravel streams or river beds? She had always wanted

soil, in many places just stones; it gave her the idea she needed.

'It was a long time before I found the gravel that I thought right for Denmans. If possible one should use gravel that blends with the walls or stonework of your house, water-worn and well-coloured, and not from an inland pit that has been graded and cut by machine.

'I find gravel gardening very accommodating

water in the garden, but water gardens of any size need so much attention that she had firmly kept that idea under control. Now she created two streams and a water hole, all without water. With the tractor she cut out the design in the grass. The 'streams' were about six feet wide and only a few inches deep, wandering down a slight southern slope for a hundred yards or so. On the highest parts she put large pieces of sandstone and ironstone from the Rother valley, and in the stream itself boulders of sandstone. Then she covered the whole area with water-worn gravel from the sea bed. 'In one place I put a large, flat, water-worn stone across to remind myself and others that it was supposed to be a stream.' The water hole through which the 'stream' flows is about thirty feet wide and circular. Around the perimeter is a low bank of soil, forming a channel which was left unplanted to emphasise the flow of water. Larger, rounded seabed stones were thrown up unevenly against the plants and bank. The planting consisted only of things that might be found growing in a dry stream bed – grasses, iris, thistles, mint, salix and sambucus. Under the banks and in the gravel everywhere were planted violets, water forget-me-nots, musk and lamiums.

The excitement did not end there. Eight years ago Joyce Robinson met John Brookes, the garden designer. It was a fortuitous encounter. She was looking for someone to take on the burden of managing the ever-evolving garden. He was seeking a place to establish his garden design school where there would be room for practical trials of his own ideas and an opportunity for his students to work in stimulating surroundings.

A dry stream of gravel is an attractive feature at Denmans

85

It has turned out to be a fruitful partnership. Together they planned and excavated a sizeable lake into which the gravel 'streams' now flow. The whole area, 3½ acres, is now garden. The general planting in the more established areas has been simplified to make maintenance easier. And to emphasise and contrast with the subtlety of the planting in the gravelled areas some swatches of brighter colour have been introduced.

The former flint and brick stable block has been converted to become John Brookes' home and studio. Here brighter colours and more exotic shapes dominate. Strong architectural plants such as large sempervivums, phormiums of several types, and cordyline palms have been used to good effect around a terraced area which links indoors and out to reduce the contrast between house and garden. John Brookes has also created a circular brick pond and a new herb garden. While this herb garden hints at the formality of the medieval apothecary's with individual herbs confined to strict rectangular blocks, the size of the blocks varies and they are disposed asymmetrically, like the paving which gives access to them. This informal formality is very pleasing.

Perhaps one of the most stylish new features at Denmans is a planted wall. Formerly of nondescript brick, Brookes wanted to increase its capacity to reflect sunlight into the thick summer cladding of foliage by lightening the colour. Since he believes that white-painted walls introduce an unnatural and harsh element into a garden, he chose to coat the brick with a wash of the palest of ripe wheatstraw yellow. It is one of those small touches which give Denmans its overall character – unusual, personal and different.

Denmans garden is open to the public from 29 March to 30 October, 10.00 to 18.00 hours, except Monday. It is open all Bank Holidays.

The dry stream culminates in a delta of slightly larger pebbles raised to form a natural-looking bar at the point of its junction with a lake

87

THE BARNES

EXCALIBUR

Rather than disturb the surrounding planting, the stump of this felled tree was carved into a regal hillside throne

BIGGAR PARK: Tree seat

At first sight, David and Sue Barnes's home resembles many other manor houses in the southern uplands of Scotland which have been given Georgian and Victorian face-lifts. The stone pillars of the gateway, the curving drive through tree-studded pastureland, the abundance of plain clipped lawn and the broad sweep of gravel fronting the house are all in keeping with its façade and conform to the eighteenth-century landscape tradition which the owners of these homes jealously fostered.

Even Tinto – the hill of fire – which dominates the vista from the house, and all the rest of the rolling Lanarkshire hills, could have been modelled by Capability Brown.

There was little that the Barnes could have done to change the general setting of their property when they bought it twelve years ago. And although they could have made drastic changes to its front aspect, they decided to leave it substantially intact, 'because it seemed appropriate'. Their major work was confined to the areas behind and flanking the house, which sits at the bottom of a fairly steeply sloping site that flattens out to form a small plateau at the top of their five acres of gardened ground.

As was inevitable with this couple who have been associated for so long with great nursery enterprises, their main concern has been with choice planting. There are many good plantsmen in gardening, but what makes the Barnes unique is both the density of their planting and the attractive and innovative way in which the plants have been used.

Only the large walled garden on the plateau, used principally for vegetable growing, had been intensively gardened by the previous owner of the house. Elsewhere there were several notable trees, including some fine beeches, all reaching maturity. Numerous evergreen yews and laurels, so enjoyed by the Victorians, had filled out into dauntingly heavy copses in several places. Many of these, particularly to the east of the house, were thinned or taken out to allow more light to reach the ground, thus enabling a great many white gean cherries, which the Barnes have planted, to prosper. In the spring they form

parasols over thick carpets of bluebells and naturalised narcissi.

To create a feeling of enclosure on the low ground, the Barnes established a large simple rectangle of mown lawn surrounded by a tightly-clipped beech hedge just to the south-east of the house. The only feature in this green basilica is a formal circular lily pond. The whole adds up to a very stylish piece of garden geometry, offering a splendid foil to the intense planting elsewhere. It's a fine place in which to brood and make plans undisturbed by the jostle of beautiful blooms competing for attention in other parts of the garden.

The west door of the house opens onto a dining terrace created from stone slabs which previously formed the floor of the old stables and

BIGGAR PARK

A House
B Paved area: 'dining terrace'
C Main entrance
D Kitchen garden

1 Morning room
2 Green court
3 Green house
4 Path of chippings
5 Bird bath
6 Statue
7 Herb garden
8 Troughs standing in pebbles
9 Lawn
10 Scree with rocky outbursts
11 Log steps
12 Tree seat
13 Terraces
14 To woodland glades
15 Arboretum
16 Orchard
17 Rose gardens
18 Planted hill bank
19 Shrubs and underplanting
20 Rosa Madame Hardy
21 Salix purpurea pendula
22 Bellicea lilac
23 Azaleas and lilies
24 Pyrus salicifoliar pendula

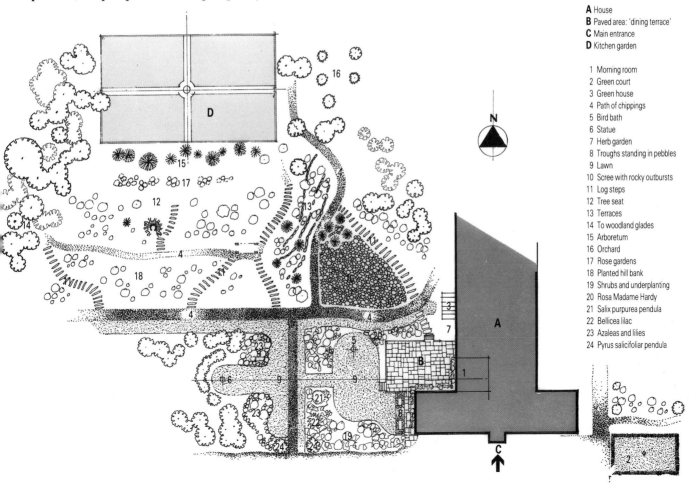

In many areas of the Biggar Park garden the Barnes have contrived a floral assault on visitors' senses. Not content with magnificent lilies, they have planted paeonies at their feet

ously formed the floor of the old stables and potting sheds. All the levels of the garden rise from the base with a low retaining wall holding back the soil of the surrounding beds. These beds are designed to offer year-round interest and have an unashamedly romantic aspect. Lilacs, azaleas, shrub roses, viburnums, philadelphus, rhododendrons, fuchsias, potentillas, and a few conifers to add winter interest are underplanted with polygonums, tiarella, prunella, gentians, violas, geraniums, acaenas and ajugas. As many lilies as possible have been crammed into the gaps between them so that in summer it is virtually impossible to see the soil beneath the thick carpet of flowers and foliage.

Dominating these beds are 'Madame Hardy' roses with strongly fragrant, pure white, very double blooms and greenish centres, looking as if they have been grown from a cutting stolen from the Garden of Eden, and a delicate *Salix purpurea* 'Pendula' – the American weeping willow – with sinuous purple-tinted wands and slender leaves.

From a point outside the morning-room window there is a vista across a lawn, over a stone chipping path, across a further patch of lawn and through a canopy of cherry trees to a female statue set in a semi-circle of palest pink and white

rhododendrons. The figure has been cunningly placed to be fully illuminated by the evening sun in summer, drawing attention to two large mixed stands of azaleas and lilies stationed on either side of the vista line behind the wings of the furthest lawn.

A broad path topped with rock chippings runs east-west along the foot of the main bank with a branch running north which climbs in gentle curves and provides the easiest route to the walled garden on the plateau.

To be able to capitalise on the southern aspect, so favourable for plant growth, the Barnes indulged in massive earthworks on the steeper areas of the bank proper. In many places the land had to be terraced to hold back soil which would have been lost to erosion once the former rough grazing was cultivated. Yards of rock walling was built to retain the earth and several long flights of steps with log risers and chipping treads were made to facilitate access to the different levels of planting.

On this newly developed area the Barnes set out to create large pools of plants of the same colour, grouped to form interlocking abstract shapes which, seen from afar, are reminiscent of the technique of 'painting with plants' on a grand scale favoured by the great Brazilian landscaper Roberto Burle Marx (see Introduction). Here again they resorted to crush planting to blanket out weed competition, reduce maintenance and create the maximum effect. Conifers of all shapes, potentillas, roses, golden cut-leafed elder, heathers, ornamental grasses, bulbs, saxifrages, hollies, sedums, saponarias, astilbes, foxgloves, colchicums, cotoneasters and many more herbaceous species all help to form this glorious display.

The whole makes a wonderful petticoat to a great thicket of species roses which skirts round the crown of the hill and is underplanted with pink and white foxgloves, artemesias, helichry-

*In the low evening light
even a tall laburnum in
full flower can't outshine
a spherical mound of
golden yew*

bright, strongly contrasting undergrowth and make a combination as stylish as you will see in any garden.

To the west of the roses are fine specimens of ornamental trees surrounding woodland glades packed with the azure-blue translucent-petalled Himalayan poppy – *Meconopsis betonicifolia*, the deep blue *M. sheldonii* and the paler *M. grandis*. Still further west there are azaleas and rhododendrons under large canopies of oak and chestnut, mixed with several types of acer and other shade-loving shrubs. In spring there are sheets of snowdrops followed by trilliums, nomocharis, notholirion with the stately *Lilium giganteum* emerging to dominate the scene in the summer. Many ferns have been planted in this area to add a cool touch.

Nearby, running out from a spinney of interesting conifers, there is a dry stone waterfall built from rock and heavy gravel to resemble the dry bed of a mountain stream. It provides pleasingly hard contrast to the thick ground cover of dark blue hardy geranium and fragile pale pink claytonia which grows about it.

On the southern edge of the plateau, just beyond the wall of the kitchen garden, there is an old orchard which in spring is carpeted with snake's-head fritillaries interspersed with large drifts of dogstooth violets. The old plum and apple trees have been used as climbing frames for clematis. Elysian meadows must have looked like this.

Almost exhausted by the climb up the hill and by the marvels seen en route, the visitor arrives at the Barnes's greatest achievement: the transformation of a one-acre walled kitchen garden into a mixed ornamental and vegetable garden of exceptional beauty. Mown grass walks along the central axis and across the middle of the plot join a path set inside the perimeter beds. They define four vegetable and soft-fruit plots. Abundant and superbly managed, these furnish the kitchen with most of its fresh produce requirements. However, walking down the two main alleys, the ornamental planting is so cunningly arranged and so intensive that a visitor is hardly aware that the walled garden contains any vegetables at all: very deep borders devoted to a mixed planting of herbaceous perennial and annual plants are backed by a screen of climbers supported on lengths of massive rope which, it is believed, was part of the tow line used to manoeuvre the *Queen Mary* after she was launched in Glasgow. The rope hangs in great swags from lines of stout posts. A circular lily pond is set in a widened circular area of lawn where the two central grass paths meet. A bronze arm with the sword Excalibur emerges from the pool to attract attention and lure visitors at the gate to investigate further.

This hub of the garden has been further emphasised by planting four pairs of fastigiate Irish yews towards the perimeter of the circle with four vigorous soft-pink double-bloomed Constance Spry roses set between and behind them. Curved bands of lower-growing, silver *Stachys lanata*, mauve erigeron and white Shasta daisies have been planted between the roses and the mown pathway. They too pull a roving eye back into the heart of the garden, though there is plenty to distract a visitor's attention, particularly in early summer when the borders make a spectacular display of pale orange geums, blue mertensias, *Veronica gentianoides* and the grey spiky plumes of Asphodels. Pyrethrums, lupins, astrantias, aquilegias and Pyrenean lilies are among later arrivals, with peonies, geraniums, erigerons, delphiniums, aconitums, veronicas, roses and anthemis following on before the phlox, day lilies, sidalcea, oenothera, and lavatera crown the high summer. Finally, pride of place is ceded to dwarf golden rod, scabious, lysimachias, thalictrums, helianthemums, nepeta, michaelmas daisies,

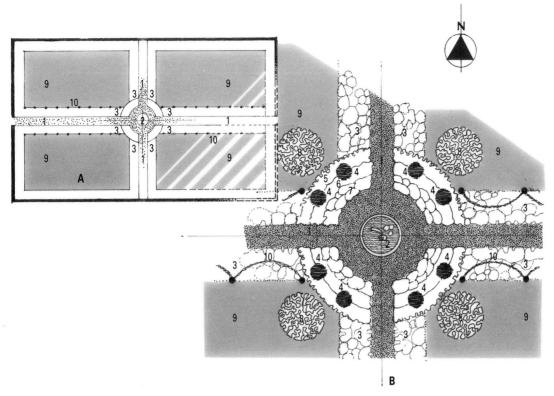

BIGGAR PARK: Kitchen garden

A Plan: walled kitchen garden
B Central axis feature

1 Lawn path
2 Water lily pond 'Excalibur feature'
3 Flower borders
4 Fastigiate Irish yews
5 White shasta daisies
6 Mauve erigeron
7 Silver stachys lanata
8 Rose 'Constance Spry'
9 Kitchen garden plots
10 Suspended rope on posts

93

An overview of the walled garden at Biggar Park shows how the four vegetable areas are hidden from sight to visitors moving between the herbaceous borders of the central allée

94

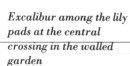

A visitor's eye view down the central allée of the walled garden

Excalibur among the lily pads at the central crossing in the walled garden

fillipendula and a host of other providers of autumn colour. Only a few of the hundreds of species which make up the glorious season-long tapestry of the herbaceous borders have been mentioned. The main aim in these beds is to avoid colour clashes.

An interesting lesson which all gardeners can learn from the herbaceous beds is the splendid way in which the larger plants are supported without any stakes being evident. Early in the season the Barnes make simple domes by bending sheets of old (and preferably rusty, because it is less evident) large-mesh sheep wire and place them over the crowns of the plants, which soon grow through and hide them.

Most of the wide borders which fringe the walled garden are devoted to large-flowering shrubs, including shrub roses underplanted with a variety of hardy geraniums. On the walls themselves are apples, pears, plums and raspberries with gooseberries, and both black and red currants also thriving in their shelter.

Stealing some of the land from the vegetables, the Barnes have also created a classical rectangular rose garden with a pure stand of hybrid teas and they are currently making a small, formal, box-edged *parterre* 'just to provide additional interest' – as if any was needed!

THE LASTS

ENNOBLING BUILDINGS

The garden at Corpusty Mill in Norfolk is a triumphant deceit. Glimpsed while passing the gate, the south façade of the linked house and watermill is typical of many in East Anglia. White and weatherboard-clad, the mill shelters climbers such as *Abutilon vitifolium*, *Magnolia delavayi*, and *Solanum crispum*. Wistaria and roses festoon the walls and ramble round the door of the house. It's a picture-postcard dream contrived by gardeners John and Roger Last to welcome and reassure visitors while, at the same time, soothing and quietening their perceptions so that they will be even more astonished, shocked and delighted by the hidden sections of the garden.

Reference to one-time milling activity at the site (which continued until 1967) has been made by cutting a short path through a shrubbery to the east of the house, breaching the retaining wall of the mill pool and making steps down to the water's edge. There, in the humid atmosphere, surrounded by gunneras and swamp cypresses and other water-lovers which the Lasts have planted, it is possible to revel in the full drama of the river Bure as it plunges over a weir. When the mill was active its roar must have masked the dull trundle of the wheel and grinding machinery. And the sound lingers in visitors' ears as, slightly taken aback by their encounter with so strong a natural force, they cross the gravel in front of the

mill and make their way through an iron gate into the garden proper. On crossing this threshold the mood changes swiftly. For although there is plenty more water featured in the garden, it appears in much calmer guises.

Tranquillity is the abiding impression in the first area of the garden, the central feature of which is an irregularly shaped mown lawn surrounded by a mixed planting of ornamental trees, shrubs and bolder herbaceous plants. A tall, creeper-clad wall – the relic of an old grain store – provides a solid boundary to the north.

Separated from the wall by a band of mixed planting, which is bisected by a small stream, is an attractive terrace feature slightly raised above lawn level and backed by a low brick wall. This incorporates a flint-lined apse with a lion's-head fountain spurting water into a low basin. The main features of the terrace are a sundial on a stone pedestal and an interesting treatment of the pavement which consists of paving slabs alternating with areas topped by bold round flints with patterns of smaller flints or herbaceous planting where the terrace has been left untopped. Set in the lawn near the terrace edge is a very conventional, small, round lily pond.

As an ensemble it is characteristic of the type of feature introduced by designers of the more luxurious type of early-twentieth-century villa garden, such as Edward Lutyens. It is notable for

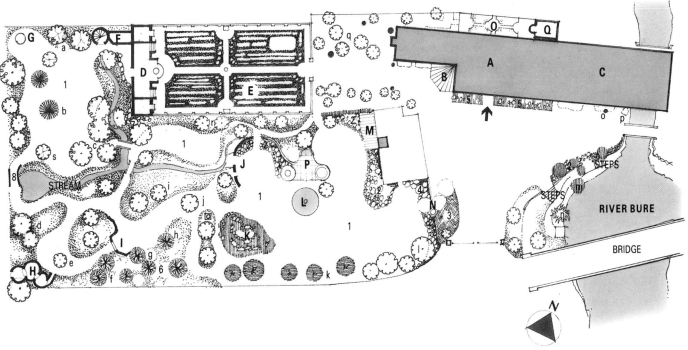

THE MILL HOUSE, CORPUSTY:
Garden Plan

A Mill house
B Conservatory
C Mill
D Pavilion
E Kitchen garden
F Tower
G Monument
H Grotto

I Gothic ruin
J Arch
K Rock garden
L Pool
M Terrace and summer house
N Gate
O Dry garden
Q Gothic greenhouse

1 Lawn
2 Borders
3 Ericas
4 Roses
5 Bedding
6 Woodland
7 Rocks
8 Bridge

a Davidia rivolucrata
b Picea breweriana
c Magnolia X veitchii
d Magnolia sargentiana robusta
e Prunus serula
f Magnolia 'Leonard Messel'
g Magnolia cordata
h Ginkeo biloba
i Metasequoia glyptostroboides
j Magnolia X soulangcana
k Cedrus deodara 'aurea'

l Prunus 'Tai-Haku'
m Taxodium distichum
n Gunnera manicata
o Magnolia grandiflora
p Campsis Madam Galen
q Cedrus atlantica 'glauca'
r Eucryphia nymansa
s Facus sylvatica 'aurea pendula'

97

There's a feel very reminiscent of Lutyens at his best in this early piece of garden masonry designed and built by the Last brothers. To avoid too much plain brick surface becoming boring, they substituted facing bricks with large flints in places and created a blind oeil de bœuf to the left of the archway to site a bust

the quality of the workmanship, but its real significance lies in the fact that it marks the site of the first attempt made by the Last brothers to alter the character of the garden by providing architectural features which they designed and built themselves.

To balance the terrace, on the southern side of the lawn they excavated a large basin down into the water table, planting ferns and other bog-loving plants at the bottom of the basin and cladding its higher outer edges with rock and gravel to make a home for plants which enjoy dry conditions. As a result this wet-and-dry garden displays a wide variety of plant forms in a small area.

Encouraged by the success of the terrace, the Lasts decided to make a higher wall along part of the western boundary of the lawn, pierced by an ambitious Roman-arched gateway and incorporating a decorative blind porthole to house a bust. This they linked to the terrace by building a curving wall of intermediate height, leaving a gateway to a path through the bed to the north. To prevent so much brickwork becoming monotonous they left out facing bricks at intervals and filled the gaps with large rounded flints.

For all its obvious attractions, the whole lawn

The first of a remarkable series of follies which the Lasts built, this simulated ruined abbey wall includes carved stones recovered from demolition sites

area of the garden is merely a foyer to the magnificent theatre hidden beyond its western boundary. This area was formerly the miller's orchard and, when the Lasts arrived at Corpusty, it contained some ancient apple and pear trees and one gnarled old horse-chestnut. Their dappled shade provided ideal conditions for the camellias, rhododendrons and magnolias which the Lasts planted. It has now developed into a mature woodland garden with an enchanting underbrush of smaller shrubs and a soft floor of hellebores, mertensias, trilliums, fritillaries and species peony. There are various species of meconopsis, too, and lilies for later summer colour, notable among them the seven-foot spires of *Cardiocrinum giganteum*.

A large, romantic pool at the western end of the orchard is fed by two small streams, one of which is fed, in turn, from the lion fountain basin and runs from behind the lawn terrace wall in an east-west direction. Enlarging what was previously a shallow drainage ditch running from north to south across the orchard area, the Lasts made this the course of the second stream. It was supplied with water (which issues from what appears to be a natural rocky spring) by digging a 100-yard feeder ditch from the river. Water from the pool flows out of the garden, into a boundary stream, and under a splendid hump-back bridge which the Lasts built, though it looks as though it was used by pack horses throughout the Middle Ages. Encrusted with bold, round flintstones and with impressive flint abutments, it was initially formed by building bricks over an arch of corrugated iron which was removed when the mortar binding the bricks had set. It makes a perfect termination to the vista in that area of the orchard.

The moist banks of the feeder streams and the pool itself – in some places heavily shaded and in others fully exposed to bright sunshine – support a wide range of marsh-loving and aquatic plants. Primulas of many kinds abound and self-seed prolifically. Hostas thrive so well that quite common varieties seem to be affected by gigantism. Yellow-spired, purple-leaved ligularias grow thicker than daisies in a lawn. Arum lilies, astilbes, rheums, rodgersias, irises and orchids all prosper. Marsh marigolds create great patches of gold lustre in spring while later the scapes of peltiphyllums make a pink haze. Skunk cabbages flourish so well that their leaves resemble banana foliage and their decadent aroma gives the poolside a slightly mysterious atmosphere.

In the south-west corner of the orchard garden lies a cavernous entrance in an impressive mound of carstone rock which they built. There the Lasts have created a baffling multi-level track through a grotto which consists of three, almost circular, domed rock chambers. It took them two winters and necessitated barrowing thirty tons of the West Norfolk gingerbread-coloured sandstone the whole length of the garden. Central occuli in the head of each dome admit an eerie light which glows green through the overhead canopy of chestnut foliage and animates the two large eighteenth-century masks of river gods which they bought to dominate the central chamber. After the shock of coming upon these, it is reassuring to peer through an irregular opening in the wall of the final chamber to view the boundary stream and the village green. The grotto conveniently masks the garden boundary where the hedge is very thin.

The sandstone, which is soft and light-coloured when quarried, darkens and hardens on aging and quickly attracts a cladding of moss and lichen, making it appear ancient. The Lasts used more of it for two other fine artefacts in the orchard garden. A division between two small glades in the thick planting was created by building what could be interpreted as a section of a wall and doorway of a ruined monastery. More

daunting but equally romantic is a twenty-foot-high tower at the head of the north-south stream. Acting as a gazebo, it contains a spiral staircase leading to a viewing platform. Parts of the interior are decorated with very convincing 'relics' of medieval wall-painting.

When they leave the orchard garden near the tower, visitors find themselves only a short step away from one of the most remarkable vegetable

Soft Norfolk carstone was used by the Lasts to build their folly tower with an upper storey which serves as a gazebo. The wall of the circular staircase has been covered with very convincing copies of medieval wall paintings

99

gardens in Britain. Formerly the grain store for the mill, it was demolished to leave standing only a large rectangle of brick walls twelve feet high. With no roof, it became the perfect site for a fully walled garden; an ideal place in which to grow vegetables and soft fruit for the house.

But the Last brothers would never be satisfied by a commonplace vegetable patch. By now they were dedicated to the notion that all areas of the garden should be ennobled by buildings, and they embarked upon their most ambitious project: a pavilion at the western end of the garden.

The taller, pedimented central portion of the pavilion has a concave 'dished' façade half surrounding a well, with an arched alcove housing the figure of a water-carrying lady clearly intent upon supplying the vegetables' most vital need. It is surmounted by an impressive dome and lantern and has smaller, flint-lined alcoves set in its walls. Separated from the central building are lower, flanking loggias which both make and store compost – one for last year's garden refuse and the other for this season's vegetable trash. Although the pavilion serves as a very superior garden shed, with the area beneath the dome used to store the barrow, mower and garden tools, it wouldn't look out of place gracing a favoured corner of the park of a Medici summer palace. Vistas through interior archways pierce and join the buildings, culminating in eye-luring statuary, and the rear walls linking the archways have been painted by John Last to show very convincing *trompe-l'œil* vases on pedestals. They take their form from an actual stone vase set centrally in the garden, the reality of which makes *them* the more credible.

The side walls of the former grain store back a shallow arcade of flinted arches with brick edging which harmonise with the materials used in the pavilion. Espaliered fruit – nectarines, peaches, morello cherries – are trained against the wall inside the arches of the arcade. A central

It is difficult to imagine that this ambitious brick and flint 'packhorse' bridge hasn't been in place for centuries. The Lasts built the basic arch using curved sheets of corrugated iron as a support

101

By building this wonderful domed garden shed to store the tools and wheelbarrow, plus 'wings' on either side in which to make compost, the Lasts turned the inside of what had been the grainstore for the mill into one of the handsomest kitchen gardens in England

102

path through the vegetable garden is gravelled and has been prettified by edging it with lavenders and herbaceous plants such as sweet williams. In the vegetable beds themselves there is no lack of novelty – the peas, for example, instead of being supported on bamboo canes or hedge twigs, climb lengths of low, decorative iron railing which are moved about each season. And since furnishing supplies of produce for the kitchen has always been considered a worthy activity, the vegetables are brought back to the house along a broad avenue flanked by tall Doric columns, reminiscent of a Roman triumphal route.

Beyond the western walls of the house the Last brothers demolished most of what was formerly a row of pigsties and a stable, creating a charming arbour from what remained. Decorated inside with a large painted panel of a lyre among bold foliage, it backs a figure of Pan in full flute among a sea of hardy geraniums and a prostrate juniper.

Lurking behind the house to the north is a secret dry garden. A small walled enclosure, it has raised beds which provide the rapid drainage enjoyed by such Mediterranean plants as yuccas, kniphofias, cistus, *Convolvulus cneorum*, *Fremontodendron 'Californian Glory'* and *Clematis armandii*. The Lasts glazed the roof of a former wash house at the eastern end of the dry garden and added a Gothic brick bay with an ogee dome, to convert it into an impressive conservatory. There is a soothing pool and fountain inside, and mounted on one of its walls is a fine alabaster reredos rescued from the demolition of a Victorian church.

On the north wall of the dry garden, from a Gothic niche backed by a *trompe-l'œil* painting of a landscape seen through an archway, a robust lion rampant surveys the scene with a gaze which suggests that he too wonders what the brothers Last will get up to next.

Lady Rosse

CASTLES AND COTTAGES

For more than half a century Anne, Countess of Rosse, has been gardening hard, using a fine blend of imagination and good taste to make delightful and indelible marks on the landscape. The creation of two gardens – Nymans in Sussex with its feeling of rare intimacy, and the majestic parklands of Birr Castle in Ireland – could alone have assured her reputation among the top rank of garden designers. But to these notable achievements must be added tiny town gardens in London and a floral haven created within the protection of the walls of what was once a kitchen garden in a bleak area of Yorkshire. And so generous has she been with her advice over the years that hundreds of other gardeners have developed outstanding features on their plots as the result of suggestions which she has made.

Lady Rosse's strength as a designer stems from what she describes as her 'love and appreciation of plants and . . . motherly understanding of their whims.' This means that in her gardens, unlike those of many more spectacular designers, the plants are so perfectly matched to their environment that they prosper to embellish and complement an already strong and stylish framework.

The features which most attract the attention of visitors to Nymans at Handcross in Sussex occupy the area immediately surrounding the house. The feeling is one of loving domesticity rather than grandeur. Considered as a whole, Nymans is like a series of small manorhouse gardens strung together, incorporating all the best features of such gardens: majestic cedars, shady alleys, palettes of smooth lawn, raised rock gardens, billowing flower-packed shrubberies, sunken rose gardens and a fine pergola walk festooned with climbing hydrangeas.

It is a place full of lessons and encouragement for more modest gardeners. Quite distinct areas are well separated from each other by hedges, walls or curtains of shrubbery or woodland, broken only by gaps or gateways sufficiently wide to allow the eye to be enticed by hints of beauty beyond.

The difference between these familiar, favourite elements at Nymans and those found in less distinguished gardens lies in the quality of the artefacts, the planning, and the subtlety with which these features have been mixed and arranged. This reflects directly the care and understanding of three generations of keen gardeners.

When Lady Rosse's grandfather, Ludwig Messel, having established himself as a banker in London, bought the property, it was a rather uninspiring Georgian house with a walled kitchen garden. Its greatest asset was some maturing woodland in the park and a few fine

By cladding the river walls with a thick curtain of colourful trailing plants at Birr Castle in Ireland, Lady Rosse transformed a forbidding medieval bastion into a charming home

specimen trees. Messel's new neighbours turned out to be people such as Gertrude Jekyll and Sir Edward Loder, and it was natural that he should have become fired by their enthusiasm for gardening, sponsoring plant-hunting expeditions to remote places and providing homes for the plants which the explorers brought back.

Lady Rosse's father, Col. Leonard Messel, displayed very little interest in gardening until he retired from the army after World War I and, in his turn, became infected by the gardening bug. While his wife exercised her talents as a decorator and designer in directing the remodelling of the house to make it one of the most charming neo-Gothic homes in England, Col. Messel, assisted by his sister Muriel, carried on with the development of the garden and became fascinated by magnolia breeding. Among the many beautiful hybrids he created, the lovely 'Leonard Messel' is perhaps the best known.

By the time that Lady Rosse inherited Nymans it had been ravaged by time and disaster. Many areas of the garden had become overgrown during World War II and a fire in 1947 had gutted a large portion of the house, including the magnificent Gothic hall. With her husband Michael, the

Sixth Earl of Rosse, she set about its rehabilitation. He was an acknowledged expert in trees and shrubs, participating in collecting expeditions and fostering the journeys of other explorers. Lady Rosse acknowledges that in that domain her husband was her mentor.

From the results which can be seen at Nymans and elsewhere they clearly made a wonderful team. To Nymans they introduced a host of fine plants, among them a great collection of camellias from Portugal, fine cypresses from Carolina and many of the best old-fashioned roses. Lady Rosse's contribution was to ensure that they were well set.

Among her achievements at Nymans, one of the most obvious has been to open up many lovely vistas over the Sussex landscape which can be viewed from and which contribute to the garden. She has also discreetly removed many barriers within the garden boundaries, making it easier to glimpse one section of the garden from its neighbour. By vigorous pollarding, pruning and total removal (all techniques which, together with the best way to root cuttings, sow seed and plant and maintain trees and shrubs, she learnt from James Comber who was head gardener when she was a child), Lady Rosse has made many vital contributions to Nymans.

Instead of demolishing the relict 'Gothic' walls of the great hall which remained after the fire, she had them reinforced to become a wonderful folly as a backdrop for climbing plants. That was certainly the sort of theatrical touch which her brother Oliver Messel would have admired. She planted the camellias from Portugal as a long thick hedge – one of the most glorious gardening sights in Britain each spring. Many of the fine vases and other masonry objects which beckon the eye towards other areas of the garden were her selection and she supervised their location. It is her happy choice of *Hydrangea arborescens* to garnish the pergola walk which makes it such a tastefully showy feature in early summer.

Work at Nymans still goes on. Visitors can now see a new bronze heron in a charming pond created for it at the base of new steps leading up to the rehabilitated mount.

If, at Nymans, Lady Rosse ever felt constricted by the achievements of her ancestors, at her husband's home, Birr Castle in County Offaly in Ireland, she was presented with an open canvas which was both a wonderful opportunity and a challenge. There is nothing remotely domestic about Birr: it is a vast medieval castle, the bastion of a fighting lord, softened in places by romantic Georgian and neo-Gothic additions. The grazing in the well-timbered park ran right up to the castle walls and, apart from the trees, the most important features were two rivers which ran through the grounds and the relics of the enormous telescope which was built in 1841 by the Third Earl. Lord Rosse's ancestors were scientists and engineers, not gardeners; notable among them was Sir Charles Parsons who pioneered the steam turbine engine. And as far as the present-day gardens at Birr are concerned, it was fortuitous that Lord Michael developed his childhood enthusiasms for trees and shrubs and married such a talented garden designer.

Tiny and delicate though she is, Lady Rosse tackled Birr with robust enthusiasm and determination. Her overall aim was to soften and beautify the immediate surroundings of the castle while respecting their park-like character; to improve the view both in the open pasture and closer woodland areas by planting the ornamental trees which her husband collected; to enrich the planting round a small lake by introducing species which would thrive in its moist environment; and to create a lovely formal garden in the vast area of land available.

The plants which Lady Rosse used to make the castle walls and flanks less forbidding; the two curving terraces which she cut into a river bank

Lady Rosse's talents as an all-round designer of great style are evident in this garden seat which she designed and which incorporates the letters A and M – the initials of her own and her husband's christian names – into the framework of its backrest

cleared of scrub yew to provide it with a decorative skirt; and the view from these terraces across the water to a veritable forest of magnolias (many of which were either bred by her father at Nymans or collected by her husband) with a carpet of primulas at their feet – all are certain to provoke delight. A dash across the park to the seclusion of the formal garden offers quite a different experience. Here the atmosphere is all delicate restraint; the covered walkways of hornbeam have a light, rococo feeling.

Elsewhere she has transformed a corner of an eighteenth-century lake into a lagoon garden with island, bridge, boathouse, weeping willow, flowering cherry and spiky conifer all so well placed as to evoke a quite oriental calm.

Apart from her major work at Nymans and Birr, Lady Rosse has created two other really noteworthy gardens. The small yard behind a London house which she converted into a flower-filled haven convinced her that 'no area of land is too small to create a good garden' whilst the medium-sized garden at Wormersley Park near Doncaster taught her that 'it is possible to garden well even on difficult soil and in a harsh climate.'

Wormersley and the tough clay at Birr were clearly challenges which Lady Rosse relished, because she has always treated gardening as a great adventure. She is also so convinced of its therapeutic value in what has otherwise been a hectic public life that she urges everyone with even the tiniest plot to take up gardening as an activity. However, she counsels people who are starting to garden on a virgin plot to look at it hard before grabbing for the spade.

'Worry about the furthest views first – try to obtain the maximum benefit from any good views beyond the garden – but remember that you mustn't rely upon them totally because someone may change them by putting up an ugly building. Once the major vistas have been determined, ensure that the planting doesn't mask them and, above all, never make the scheme too fussy. Adopt a very definite theme and stick to it,' she

Instead of demolishing the walls of the great hall at Nymans after it had been gutted by fire, Lady Rosse decided to use them as a highly romantic support for climbing plants

advises. She extends this dictum to particular areas like borders which, she says 'should never become a spotty patchwork. They are much more effective if each plant is used in very bold irregular clumps.' Scale, too, she feels is very important.

The greatest lesson which her experience has taught her is that gardeners should be courageous. 'Try those plants which you are not quite certain about. But if they don't provide the effect which you desire, don't be afraid to move them or abandon them altogether,' she urges.

'The main thing is to try to emulate nature as nearly as possible. Remember that you can make a beautiful garden anywhere – on a balcony or in a small back yard – in the cold and difficult north or the balmy south – no matter how improbable the site, it is always worth the effort.'

Birr Castle is at Birr in County Offally west of Dublin and is open from spring to autumn, every year, as is Nymans which is situated at Handcross in West Sussex.

*One of the most stylish
features at Birr Castle is
this hornbeam tunnel
which is reminiscent of
rococo masonry*

109

FANTASY

*Myles Challis created
this squib-humoured
horned angel to warn
visitors to his tropical
garden at Leytonstone in
East London of the
surprises in store for
them*

JACK LENOR LARSEN

AFRICA ON LONG ISLAND

A little less than one hundred miles from New York City is Roundhouse, designer Jack Lenor Larsen's Long Island house and garden. A weekend in this 27-acre hidden garden is the perfect antidote to the highly charged lifestyle of the 'Big Apple'. Instead of the wail of sirens and the squealing wheels of racing taxis, night sounds here are soothing ones – the glottal songs of frogs about the ponds, crickets in concert, and the intermittent high-pitched chirps of the cicadas. The sense of remoteness one feels in this garden is heightened by powerful suggestions of an even more distant location: the far-away continent of Africa.

The fantasy of being far removed from the frenzy of the workaday world begins in an entrance drive of sand-coloured pebbles that winds through a jungle of vegetation. Where the drive swells to a parking area, first-time visitors park their car, get out, and look around. They are surrounded by dense plantings of ferns, pygmy bamboo, azaleas, rhododendron, viburnum, and white-paper birch. Hardy and perfectly suited to the Long Island climate, this rich mixture of natives and exotics has the sort of lush density and rich interplay of textures that suggests a far more southerly location. Beyond these plantings is woodland and, half engulfed in trees, shrubs, and bamboo, an African house.

It takes some looking to find the path to the front door. It is a mere parting of the luxuriant planting of ivy, ferns, and tall bamboo canes in the densely planted entrance garden that acts as a barrier between the house and the outside world. The flagstone path is a narrow bridge across to a private world. Visitors who come in twos or more cannot walk abreast but have to enter in single file. Only a little imagination is necessary to fill in the missing elements of the

The entrance walkway to Roundhouse, Jack Lenor Larsen's Long Island retreat, cuts through ivy, bamboo and ferns

African picture: porters with head baggage, lions in the tall-grass savannah.

Jack Lenor Larsen's fascination with Africa began early in his life. 'When I was a little boy in Canada,' he relates, 'I saw an early documentary of Princess Elizabeth touring the West African colonies.' In 1960, he made the trip himself, visiting West and South Africa. What made a lasting impression upon him was the architecture. 'It was even more varied than I thought it was.' Particularly appealing was the African compound, a composite of several structures with outdoor work- and living-spaces. 'In the polygamous societies, each wife has a house – adolescent boys get a little house and the outdoor spaces are all part of it.'

In the nineteen-sixties, when he found the Long Island property, he says, 'I was interested in a personal house and a rural house.' In his desire for self-expression in his house and garden he was to draw on his memories of Africa. At that time the construction of lookalike suburban tract houses was well underway in the Hamptons. Others, he remembers, 'were buying old mills and barns and achieving rusticity that way . . . but I wanted a *personal* house.'

This desire found expression in the construction of an African-style compound with a series of houses and interrelated outdoor spaces for living and working. The main house is round, white stucco, with a dark-brown cone-shaped roof. Two smaller, round, hut-shaped houses adjoin the main house: one is a guest house; the other, called 'the silk house' because it was once Mr Larsen's studio, is now a summer living room. As on an African compound, all the buildings are connected by a large patio and exterior passages. As a concession to the New York climate, however, the houses are also joined by interior passages.

The buildings straddle a line between woodland and meadow. The land, explains Mr Larsen,

was 'only abandoned as a farm at the turn of the century – unlike other properties which were no longer farmed after the Civil War. The whaling industry died out, the train came out here, and cheap produce from the Midwest wiped out the farmers.' Those properties given up right after the War are now completely wooded. Because his land had been farmed longer, he says, only half was wooded and 'the property still had meadows and was rolling . . . It was gorgeous land.'

The entrance to the house is on the woodland side where the vegetation is quite thick and lush and where the light is subdued. On the entrance side, with its driveway and parking area, the cluster of buildings seems to join together as a barrier against the outside world. Windows are pig-eye small. The narrow path slicing through thick vegetation leads to a rather forbidding door of dark tropical-looking wood as the sole visible entryway. Sheathed in copper and studded with enormous nails, the door was designed by Mr Larsen, but looks like it might once have opened into the lair of an eighteenth-century slave trader.

The door opens, not into a dark interior, but into a house that is bright and airy. Light streams in from the garden side, where the main house and outbuildings are wide open to the outside with skylights, large windows, and glass doors. So open to the garden is the interior that the entrance and front of the house function as mere garden walls behind which the interior blends right into the garden. Paved work- and living-spaces extend outside into a vast, sunlit space.

Directly outside all the doors on the garden side is a long, semi-circular stone patio that connects all of the buildings. It has been furnished for outdoor living with tables and chairs and places for basking in the sun. Herbs billow out of small spaces amongst the stones. A wistaria grows up over the main house, providing foliage to shade the skylights in summer. Clambering

113

The narrow path to the front door slices through a lush ground cover of bamboo, ivy and ferns. Visitors must walk in single file

114

over the guest house is a trumpet vine.

Low, curving walls around the terrace give a feeling of enclosure without blocking the view. At one end of the terrace there is a small, round garden, enclosed within circular walls. Like the mud walls of Africa, constructed to keep out wandering cattle, the outsides of the walls are incised in simple linear patterns.

'These walls have worked very well. Originally there was only a terrace,' says Larsen. 'Walls create micro-climates. Now, in the circular garden,' he says, 'there is always something in bloom.'

Walls also create rooms. Around a perfectly circular pool are segments of circular wall. About five feet tall, they serve to contain and camouflage the flotsam and jetsam of swimming pool paraphernalia. While they keep discordant elements out of view from the outside, they also create a wonderfully cozy space within which there is ample room for rows of lounge chairs, a dining table and chairs and a large community of potted red geraniums. Openings in the walls lead to the terrace and to two other outdoor dining areas.

Beyond the terrace and swimming pool walls a vast, irregular oval of lawn stretches to a pond. What looks like an outdoor safari camp has been set up under awning on the lawn. Two chairs and two Indian rope beds, strung with woven plastic strips to make them weatherproof, face the pond. Mr Larsen calls this 'a reviewing stand for the croquet court.' It is also a good spot to dry off after a dip in the pool or to keep watch for alligators.

Once this spacious lawn was meadow. 'I was never going to mow the meadow,' remembers Mr Larsen. It was one of the features he found most appealing about the property. In fact, the first improvement made on the property, 'while the house was still in the planning stage,' was to provide the meadow with a pond. However, once the house and the terrace were completed, it was found that tall grasses obscured the view of the pond. As lovely as the meadow was, the pond won out as the preferred feature. 'I got a tractor and laid out beds with it,' says Larsen. He has been pleased with the choice and considers the pond, now 25 years old, his favourite part of the garden.

Despite the fact that the pond is very large and

has a central island, Mr Larsen claims 'there is virtually no maintenance. Keeping the edges of the vinyl [liner] covered,' is all that has to be done. 'It was the first time [1962] that vinyl had been used for a decorative pond,' he explains of its construction. 'Before that it was used only for irrigation ditches and reservoirs.'

A quarter of a century ago, he planted the pond with sacred lotus, despite having been told that the lotus would never flower so far north. Eight years later it began to flower – big, white blooms edged in pink – and has done so every succeeding year. By midsummer, the lettuce-green leaves of the white lotus cover a large portion of the water surface and the pond is a rich mixture of textures and luminous greens. Bright spots of blue are provided by the mass of water pickerel which blooms around the stepping stones to the island. Along the pond's edges are reeds and rushes and occasional clumps of maiden grass, *Miscanthus sinensis* 'Gracillimus'. From the house, the water and lush vegetation suggest a bend in a great, slow-moving African river.

This impression was heightened by the addition, a few years ago, of a second pond behind the first. The new pond, further from the house, is set with smooth, black river-stones and rimmed by reeds, *Miscanthus*, and cat's-tails.

Between, and overlooking, both ponds is a rustic log structure with a fire pit. 'I call it a folly,' explains Mr Larsen. 'It is where we have coffee and brandy after dinner around an open fire. Slowly it is being covered with yellow trumpet vine.' The folly owes its existence to some of Mr Larsen's favourite plants, his bamboos. 'Someone wanted some bamboo and I asked, what will you trade? They traded logs for bamboo . . .'

Bamboos are plants Larsen feels are under-valued and under-used. 'People are afraid of bamboo,' he says, adding that 'all one has to do to contain it is mow around it.' Unlike some plants which need to be cut back throughout the growing season, bamboo, he says, need only be confined for about four weeks.

Beyond the ponds, the lawn narrows and curves out of sight of the house. Suddenly there are rocks too carefully arranged, and a strange trio of maples, too bizarrely upright. Three giant Thai basket totems ten feet tall are suspended in mid-air to form a votive 'V'. It is a sacred grove. Walking through, visitors experience a sense of

Stepping stones lead to an island in the old pond

discovery and awe not unlike exploring the ruins of an ancient temple.

'In Thailand,' says Larsen, 'basket totems are used on temple grounds for fate festivals.' When strung with silk ribbons they are an indication that mirth and levity will be allowed near the temple. Sometimes, when Larsen throws a large party, he has guests enter via the exit drive and come into the garden through this grove.

Sculptures, like the basket totems, are a frequent and welcome addition throughout the garden. Their presence invites and rewards exploration. At the extreme edge of the garden a wide swathe of lawn passes between dense plantings of rhododendrons, azaleas, bulbs, and hydrangeas. Life-sized stalagmite shapes rise out of a bed of azaleas, looking like the habitations of African ants. Called 'Aspergi' by potter Jim Owen, they are composed of a combination of clay mixed with fibre glass that has been fired.

Elsewhere there are great stone balls, the work of sculptress Grace Knowlton, and a massive wooden version of the Brooklyn Bridge by Claus Burry. There are also natural sculptures harvested from the woods. 'We had a lot of dead cedar,' explains Larsen. Some of these dead trees have been planted in a part of the garden where their sun-bleached, sinewy trunks and jagged branches evoke a ghost forest. They are especially effective against a hedge of hemlock.

'It's a kind of landscape sculpture,' says Larsen of another product of the surplus of dead cedar. In the Red Garden, so called because all the azaleas and foliage are red, cedar posts have been painted Chinese red and arranged in converging lines. The intervals and heights of the posts have been adjusted to heighten perspective. At the apex formed by the posts is a sculpture, a large jug. Executed by Toshiko Takeazu, it is her largest hand-built piece. It was especially constructed and fired for outdoor use and, so far, has endured fifteen winters.

The luxury of space – 27 acres of it – allows each of these sculptures and constructions to be appreciated by itself; different moods and themes can be sustained in various parts of the garden because they are isolated from each other.

A cluster of giant, brown-glazed water jugs set the mood for an outdoor dining room that resembles a miniature Mughal garden. Set between rows of pollarded plane trees, a small cloth-walled *paradari* occupies a water throne. This dining pavilion was designed by Bill Moss. The cloth walls are made of 'Moonbeam', one of Mr Larsen's creations. It is a solar cloth that was designed to reflect heat. 'It keeps the dining pavilion warmer than the surrounding area,' says Larsen. More interesting to him, however, is the cloth's ability to reflect and augment candle light.

A quarter century of working, designing and planting has created an unforgettable garden of many moods and spaces. Now it is full: there are about 30,000 daffodils planted and no fewer than five outdoor dining spaces – not counting the folly for 'after dinner coffee and brandy.' There are two ponds, a swimming pool, and a channelled stream through the Mughal garden.

'I get joy out of gardening,' states Jack Lenor Larsen, 'because it is faster than building. I like my false sense of working somewhat spontaneously. I particularly like the destructive aspects of gardening, the clearing of trees to make views and the heading up of trees. I enjoy the illusion of working quickly.'

Gardening to Jack Lenor Larsen is an active process. The years have been spent in building up the garden. Now he is planning to sell Roundhouse because, he says, 'it is finished.' The planning and construction of a second house and garden, Longhouse, are already underway. The house is still in the planning stage, but the pond has already been dug.

*A folly with a fire-pit
is a romantic spot for
after-dinner coffee and
brandy. It overlooks the
new pond, laid with
black river stones*

117

MYLES CHALLIS

JUNGLE IN WALTHAMSTOW

Myles Challis is a leaf fanatic, perhaps the best living exponent of the possibilities of gardening with exotic foliage rather than with the more conventional items of the gardener's palette. It would not be true to say that he is opposed to flowers as such, but his preference is for unusual combinations of temperate shrubs and trees: foliage, deep, dark mysterious; foliage flecked by the sun; foliage falling in fantastic abundance.

Myles Challis's interest in foliage began when, as a boy, he collected plants for the small conservatory which flanked his parents' Hampstead home. For his fourteenth birthday, his father offered to provide heating for the conservatory, enabling him to stock it with an unusual collection of sub-tropical plants. Some he bought, and others were sent to Hampstead by an uncle who was a keen collector of tropical butterflies and had travelled extensively in the Far East in pursuit of his hobby. The uncle was no botanist, so the collection was catholic in its variety. Before long, Myles Challis's remarkable conservatory attracted attention from mature collectors – but it all came to an end when the oil crisis of the early 1970's sent heating costs beyond all reasonable limits. The conservatory could no longer be heated and the tender plants were dispersed to institutions which could afford to keep them in the temperatures to which they were accustomed.

The question was, what to do next? A great source of inspiration to Myles Challis at this time was a book he found in the Royal Horticultural Society Library called *A Gloucestershire Wild Garden*. Written in 1903 by Henry Cooke, a retired tea-planter home from India, it describes how an area of about two and a half acres had been filled with a variety of plants, some tropical, some sub-tropical and some temperate, all designed to evoke the exotic atmosphere of India in the Cotswolds. To call it 'a jungle in Gloucestershire' would perhaps be putting it too strongly, but the palms, banana trees and bamboos were unique in their profusion and in the flamboyance of their planting.

Myles Challis set out to create for himself something of the same atmosphere that the Edwardian tea-planter had so uniquely striven for in Gloucestershire. (Incidentally, some years later, his predecessor's garden provided the inspiration for the film *The Assam Garden*.) Challis bought a house in Leytonstone – an eastern suburb of London, a most unlikely place to find a jungle. It is a small Victorian villa, with a tiny strip of garden to the rear, bounded on one side by the neighbour's garden and on the other by a high wall running down the side of a narrow lane. At the far end of the garden is another high wall, so that the total effect is of a tiny secret space; it is

MYLES CHALLIS: Garden Plan

A House
B Footpath
C Pond
D Seat

High level trees to provide shade:
E Acer velutinum vanvoxemii
F Betula tristis
G Robinia frisia
H Aesculus inpica
I Populus lascicarpa
J Paulownia tomentosa
K Ailanthus altissima
L Cercidophyllum japonicum

1 Gunnera manicata
2 Peltiphyllum peltatum
3 Petasites gigantea
4 Lysichitum americanum
5 Primula florindae
6 Astilbe rivularis
7 Bamboo: Sasa palmata
8 Inula magnifica
9 Ginger: Hedychium gardnerianum
10 Banana: Musa ensete
11 Bamboo: Phyllostachys nigra
12 Blechnum tabulare
13 Ligularia veitchiana
14 Palm: Trachycarpus fortunei
15 Tree fern: Dicksonia antarctica
16 Ricinus zanzibariensis
17 Rheum tanguticum
18 Hosta sieboldiana elegans
19 Crambe cordifolia
20 Ligularia desdemona
21 Datura cornigera
22 Rodgersia tabularis
23 Corylus maxima purpurea
24 Heracleum mantegazzianum
25 Actinidia kolomitka
26 Canna wyoming
27 Vitis coignetiae
28 Melianthus major
29 Phormium tenax purpureum
30 Hydrangea aspera
31 Cornus alba elegantissima
32 Cotinus coggyria 'Royal purple'
33 Viburnum rhytidophyllum
34 Bamboo: Phyllostachys aurea
35 Actinidia chinensis

119

MYLES CHALLIS:
Chelsea Garden

1 Phormium tenax purpureum
2 Datura suaveolens
3 Aralia elata variegata
4 Banana: Musa basjoo
5 Trachycarpus fortunei
6 Acer negundo variegata
7 Corylus maxima purpurea
8 Peltiphyllum peltatum
9 Facus sylvatica pendula 'weeping beech'
10 Banana: Musa ensete
11 Dicksonia antarctica
12 Zantedeschia aethiopica
13 Arundo donax variegata

entered by a simple wooden door in the wall a few feet behind the house. Apart from its sheltered walls, the garden was quite unsuited to the purpose intended, and the soil had to be extensively treated and fertilised. Once this had been done, Myles Challis set about creating his jungle – in a space only 30ft by 40ft.

He is convinced that every garden, as well as having a profusion of foliage, should have water. The sound of falling water, and the contrast between a placid pool and the excitement of its leafy surroundings, are essential in his scheme of things. He planned a small pool beneath the far wall, with a stone seat beside it where he could sit, in the Marvel tradition, and have green thoughts in a green shade. 'I always try to persuade people to have water in their gardens. Once they have done so, they will never want to be without it.'

Another of Challis's convictions was that it would be possible to find exotic plants that were hardy enough to survive much of the year out of doors in London. He believes that, in poor weather, the evergreen qualities of foliage have

much more to offer than the conventional British lawn and herbaceous border. His leafy solution extends the season of contrast of growth from early May, after the frosts, until well into autumn, long after the familiar floral offerings have faded. Here in Leytonstone his particular choice of plants is about 75 per cent hardy and 25 per cent tender; the latter have to be taken into a conservatory in winter. The proportion could, of course, be varied to taste.

Among the tender plants is an Abyssinian banana, probably unique in Britain. There are palms, a ginger, rice-paper plants, a castor-oil plant and a half-dozen more. These include the datura which, though tender, has a surprising ability to survive. The hardier plants include a foxglove tree, an Indian horse-chestnut, a Chinese poplar, and our umbrella tree. The overall impression is one of amazing fecundity, ripeness, growth and of contrasts of texture, colour and size. Myles Challis believes in freedom of growth and size, allowing plants to reach their natural extent, and has no sympathy for those who want to cut and trim – the 'anti-size brigade,' he calls them.

Another powerful impression which the garden evokes is one of mystery, surprise – what shall we find next? Small though the area is, because of the size of the individual plants and the careful planting, there is no opportunity to 'take in' the garden as a whole. It unfolds itself: a winding stone path progresses towards the pool which is concealed until the last moment, though the sound of trickling water grows ever louder. This is a novel variation on the 'room' theory of garden design; here, instead of passing from one 'room' to another, the garden is filled with one surprise after another.

Having created his jungle in Leytonstone, Myles Challis has concentrated over the past few years on the opportunities he now has for proselytising about gardening. He calls it 'education'.

He believes firmly that it is the duty of the gardening establishment to educate the gardening public in new ways of gardening, so that traditional styles can be left behind. In 1981 he wrote his first article for the *RHS Journal*. Five years later, he exhibited at the Chelsea Flower Show for the first time. Soon he will do so again, with a remarkable all-gold garden – not golden-rod, but golden foliage in all its amazing variety. Myles Challis is not anti-flower, but he admits that he is something of a flower snob, choosing esoteric varieties, such as *Hydrangea sargentiana*, which are exotic but not 'gaudy' (a word he uses to describe the more conventional British garden colouring). The education process continues, and Myles Challis has now written his first book to bring home to us all the delights that can be derived from the foliage garden.

121

By carefully selecting hardy plants with a distinctly exotic appearance as well as genuinely tropical plants which he moves indoors in the winter, Myles Challis has made a small yard in Leytonstone resemble a patch of Burmese jungle

A SELECTION OF THE PLANTS TO BE FOUND IN MYLES CHALLIS'S GARDEN

TENDER PLANTS

Abyssinian banana	*Musa ensete*	Umbrella tree	*Magnolia tripetaca*
Palm	*Trachycarpus fortunei*	Hydrangeas	*Hydrangea aspera*
Ginger	*Hedychium gardnerianum*		*Hydrangea sargentiana*
Rice-paper plant	*Tetrapanax papyriferus*	Ligularias (various)	
		Rodgersias (various)	
		Hostas (various)	
Angel's trumpet	*Datura cornigera*	Bamboos	*Sasa palmata*
Castor oil plant	*Ricinus gibsoni (Knightii)*		*Phyllostachys nigra*
			Phyllostachys aurea
Tree fern	*Dicksonia antarctica*		
Purple Canna	*Canna generalis 'Wyoming'*	**POND-SIDE PLANTS**	
		Gunnera manicata	
Melianthus	*Melianthus major*	*Lysichitum sp.*	
		Peltiphyllum peltatum	
HARDY PLANTS		*Petasites gigantea*	
Foxglove tree	*Paulownia tomentosa*	*Astilbe rivularis*	
Indian horse-chestnut	*Aesculus indica*	*Polygonum cuspidatum spectabile*	
Chinese poplar	*Populus lasiocarpa*	*Polygonum sachalinense*	

THE FEILDINGS

BOXING THE YEW

In 1919, Percy Feilding received a telegram from his friend Lady Ottoline Morrell saying, 'Marvellous Elizabethan house for auction near here. Come at once. Morrell, Garsington.' He did as he was told, the house was bought before auction, and two years later Feilding, who was an architect, embarked on the construction of the garden.

It is not, as is sometimes said, an Elizabethan garden, but a topiary garden which takes its inspiration from the so-called 'mathematical' style of the eighteenth century. Today the garden is fully developed and its great stylishness, originally conceived in 1921, is now evident, having been nurtured by Percy's son Basil and continued by Basil's widow, Mrs Peggy Feilding.

Beckley Park was indeed a park, first enclosed in the twelfth century by Richard, Duke of Cornwall, who stocked it with deer which are still there today. The park was Crown property until it passed into private hands in the seventeenth century. The house, originally the hunting lodge, is of red brick with three towers on the garden side. Remarkably it is unaltered and unmodernised and, since it stands somewhat lost in the midst of the wild Otmoor countryside, only reached up an unmade-up track, visitors can well be excused for believing themselves back in the Elizabethan age.

As soon as one enters the gardens, the sense of the past is replaced by the overwhelming impression that one is in a fantasy or dream world. This is not because the gardens are overgrown or unkempt, for, despite the fact that the three gardeners employed by the original Mr Feilding are now no more, Mrs Feilding has maintained the grounds and the topiary in very good shape. Rather, the feeling of mystery undoubtedly results from the way in which the strong formal designs are combined in such an asymmetrical or 'unbalanced' style.

There are three groups of topiary gardens. The first is entered from an arch to the left of the house-front and is a kind of avenue of tall shapes about 100 feet in length. At the end, a hedge arch on the right leads into a diamond-shaped garden with formal edging about two feet high topped by pyramids of box. The yew boundary is high and, in parts, fourteen feet wide. The third garden area is circumscribed by the inner moat, the outer moat forming a sort of boundary to the garden within the park.

The original box planting was made by Percy Feilding but he died seven years later and never saw the scheme fully developed. He planted *Buxus sempervivens* and *Buxus balearica* (bluer, with a larger leaf than common box), some eighteen inches high in a rich clay. The curious series of cones, spheres and pyramids he must have read about in architectural studies of the eighteenth century, when they replaced the earlier ornate topiary of animals and birds, which were disliked and satirised much as garden gnomes are today. Alexander Pope, for example, pretended that he had for sale 'a quick-set hog, shot up into a porcupine, by being forgot a week in rainy weather'. By some curious quirk of fate there is now at Beckley a peacock and a sort of seated teddy bear in the first garden, but Mrs Feilding admits that this may well have been 'a mistake'. It is all too easy to develop mistakes in topiary culture by a slip of the shears.

The original planting was done in the spring and clipped two or three years later; ideally, the

Despite his colossal size, this leafy bruin seems too cuddly to be intimidating, and serves as amusing relief in a garden in which many of the topiary forms are geometric

123

box should have been clipped twice a year since. However, since Mr and Mrs Feilding took over the garden, this has never been possible. Mrs Feilding recalls with some amusement a questionnaire received from the Box Society of America which asked:

How often do you fertilise?
How often do you replace?
How often do you apply growth retardents?

The answer to all the questions was 'never'. No doubt the Society would have been surprised, too, to learn that the plants are clipped only once a year in the frost-free period between May and September. The box edgings were thinned after the war in order to narrow the hedges and now they average two feet by fourteen inches with about 5 feet of space between the pyramids. The tall yew is cut by electric trimmers from a scaffolding, although the fourteen-foot-wide outer edging is strong enough to crawl along and this is sometimes the method used. All new growth is cut off, and the size and shape retained by an all-round clip done in stages.

In the garden itself the extraordinary shapes of the topiary command attention, but they are not its only stylish feature. For example, as one passes from the first garden to the second, up a bank in the shrubbery ahead comes a nymph chasing a faun, the latter looking somewhat startled by the encounter. This is a piece of sculpture acquired by Mrs Feilding, the work of Westmacott, probably Sir Richard Westmacott who died in 1856 and is buried at Chastleton not far away. By locating the statue in such an informal setting, it attracts much more interest than if it had been dumped at the base of a yew.

124

Right: Geometric topiary was the obvious choice for a garden to surround a genuinely unspoilt Tudor hunting lodge (which is pictured here in the 1920s and on the far right in the 1980s)

Far right: Stout square-cut hedges, pyramids and spheres make splendid guardians at Beckley Park and provide the most dramatic effects in low, early morning or late evening sunlight

At Beckley Park nature has been contorted to wonderful effect by clipping, creating fascinating secret areas like this one seen from a window in the house

126

The area enclosed by the inner moat is a trim lawn with flagstone paths edged by castellated 'battlements': pyramids and spheres all in box. At the corners are hornbeam 'houses' and, where the inner moat becomes visible (part of the moat has been filled in, though its 'line' remains), its slope is covered in a cascade of moisture-loving plants such as gunneras. Another of Mrs Feilding's additions in this area is an old climbing rose from Kiftsgate which she is training up a yew. Although the three moats delineate the shape of the garden, they are all largely filled in. Mrs Feilding acknowledges, however, that her father-in-law probably intended to 'do something about them' had he lived long enough.

Beckley is unique, not in having a garden of intense topiary but in the dense and fantastical style with which the design has been developed. It has certainly influenced other gardeners, whether they have merely 'fantastified' an existing box or yew into a curiously dream-like or surreal shape, or whether they have used tubbed or potted box in an unusual way. After Mrs Feilding's death, the house will go to the English Heritage Trust, so there is every reason to hope that this extraordinary exercise in topiary dreamwork may long continue to be with us.

The lessons to be learnt from Beckley Park topiary gardens include the following:

(i) Topiary does not take centuries to grow to great heights

(ii) Box does not require extensive upkeep

(iii) Box need not be cut in the traditional formal lines emphasising perspective.

(iv) Topiary does not have to match the period of the house; it is ageless. The imagination of the cutter is the most important factor. The only rule is 'cut with style'.

Arrangements to see this garden can be made by prior correspondence with Mrs Feilding.

R. J. DYKES

TROPICS IN NEW ORLEANS

Like every other house on the street, The R. J. Dykes residence in New Orleans' French Quarter presents a rather bland, correct façade to the world. There isn't even a shade tree on its plain street-side. The only indication of any interest in horticulture whatsoever is that someone has taken a great deal of trouble to punch a hole through the concrete sidewalk. In it a single but very robust four o'clock plant has grown to ample proportions. Otherwise there is absolutely no hint of the extraordinary garden completely hidden from the street.

Walking into that lush and opulent garden behind the house, then, is a pleasant shock. One has the sensation of having suddenly entered an enormous greenhouse in which every niche from ceiling to floor is occupied by plants. Upright, tall, broad, creeping, hanging, cascading – plants of every description fill every inch of space. The greenhouse effect is enhanced by foliage-clad fences, walls, and buildings all around as well as the ceiling of plants overhead. In fact, the very air exudes a rich mixture of musty earth and flower fragrances, suggestive of hothouse.

Like most New Orleans gardens, this one boasts a respectable collection of Indica azaleas, gingers, a tea olive, bananas and a Merleton vine. Unlike most others, it doesn't stop there but takes full advantage of a nine-month growing season, rich alluvial soil, generous rains, and a hothouse climate for seven months of the year. Instead of concentrating on traditional plants and lawn which have to be beaten back incessantly in New Orleans, R. J. Dykes has made optimum use of the propitious climate with an atypical mixture of tropicals, semi-tropical plants, mild climate ornamentals, vegetables, perennials, and annuals.

'We can get most plants – I've tried to use just about everything that will do in this area. It's tropical in New Orleans until December, January, and February,' says Dykes. 'The climate supports an immense variety of plant life.'

His exuberant collection grows in rich profusion in a garden given over entirely to beds joined by a network of stone paths. Sheets of Spanish moss hang from a large sweet olive. Beneath and around it are plants familiar to more northerly latitudes: a peach tree, hollies, nandina, liriope, day lilies, iris. These, in turn, mingle with the trusty standbys of the New Orleans climate: gingers, bananas, and crinums. Elsewhere are citrus, sago palms, a large avocado, and tropicals: cycads, orchids and bromeliads. There is a well-stocked vegetable garden which produces three crops each year.

A delightfully spontaneous mixture fills the garden, looking not messy, but wonderfully like a

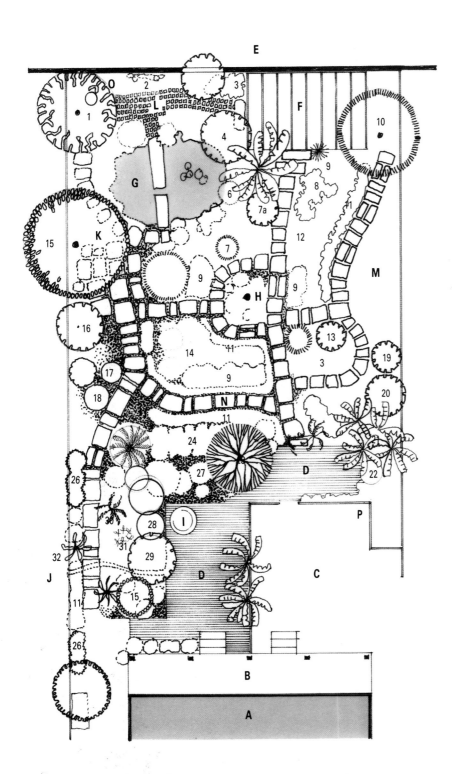

R. J. DYKES:
New Orleans Garden Plan

A House
B Porch
C Private Courtyard
D Brick patio
E Brick building. Height 20'0"
F Greenhouse
G Goldfish pond
H Martin house
I Well
J French runnel drain
K Sitting area
L Cobblestone area
M Summer vegetable area
N Stone path
O Sculpture
P Wooden fence

1 Cherry laurel
2 Espalier citrus
3 Montbretia
4 Candlestick tree
5 Banana
6 Palm
7a Plum
7 Nandina
8 Asparagus
9 Iris
10 Peach Tree
11 Liriope
12 Seasonal vegetables with mint and wild strawberries
13 Tree hydrangea
14 Violets, mint and wild strawberries
15 Sweet olive
16 Japanese magnolia
17 Urn with geranium
18 Camellia
19 Althea
20 Sweet bay magnolia
21 Giant banana
22 Urn with ginger and impattens
23 Acassia
24 Crinum
25 Sago palm
26 Holly screen
27 Azalea
28 Camellia
29 Avocado
30 Hidden lily
31 Aspidistra
32 Ginger

129

In good years, when there is little winter frost, bananas will continue to grow in R. J. Dykes' jungly garden in the French Quarter of New Orleans. Apart from welcome fruit, they offer the shade essential for an escape from the burning summer sun

130

jungle. Making their way through the garden on the stepping stones set high above the moist 'muck', and surrounded by so many dense layers of foliage, visitors might easily lose their way.

This year, says Dykes, the garden is even more lush and profuse than usual. 'This year we didn't have a freeze . . . only one little snap that went to thirty [degrees Fahrenheit] and didn't affect anything.'

Plants that take more than one season to produce fruit or blooms, like the pink-shell gingers or the giant banana, are in their full glory. This year they have justified their existence. 'Now the giant banana is twelve inches in diameter and two storeys high – and loaded with bananas.'

'This is where the semi-tropicals come in,' says Dykes, explaining that sometimes it won't freeze for several years running; at other times frost is regular. A New Orleans gardener will bring along certain plants for years in the hopes of just such a frostless period. 'When I plant them, I try to put them in one area – not like a permanent thing. Most people do it this way.'

Even when frost is regular, the moist, sunny New Orleans climate supports vigorous growth. Bananas grow to twelve feet in the first two months of spring. The cypress vine (*Ipomoea quomoclit*), after freezing to the ground, will come up and totally cover a small tree in a single season. Of 'fine, fine, fine' texture, the cypress vine has 'little bitty red flowers.' This year, says

By clever use of tender subjects in pots as well as hardier plants in the ground, R. J. Dykes has managed to incorporate an astonishing range of foliage types and flowers in such a small garden

Dykes, 'it looks like somebody's melted something red and poured it all over the Japanese magnolia.'

'The big sagos stay out – they're in the ground. Sago palms do very well in New Orleans,' he explains, adding, 'they'll even grow on the other side of Lake Pontchartrain in Baton Rouge. The fronds freeze but the trunk never freezes.' One of Dykes' sago palms is about a hundred years old. 'I picked that up out of the dumpster. Someone was throwing it away. I knew it was alive.'

Plants, like the stepping stones in the garden, have come from 'here, there and around' and sometimes even from the city dump.

Another plant that appears dead after frost is the ginger. 'Butterfly gingers freeze absolutely to the ground every year . . . and will bloom every year,' explains Dykes. Those that need two years to bloom are good foliage plants in New Orleans – with or without frost.

Another 'good southern plant' is the sweet olive (*Osmanthus fragrans*). Its 'teeny, bitty white flowers' cover the tree and give off a fragrance that you can 'smell for two blocks' says Dykes, adding, 'sometimes the whole quarter is fragrant.' Another variety, called the 'tea olive', has larger blooms that Dykes considers to be 'maybe a little sweeter.'

The *Cassia*, a dependable plant in New Orleans, has outdone itself this year, having spread twenty feet over patio and paths. Dykes likens walking under it to being under 'one of those tropical trees with many trunks – a banyan – that spreads out overhead.' It starts blooming in October and will continue until the first frost. He describes its appearance as 'an umbrella of yellow.'

For all of its lush growth, this garden is only eight years old. Before that, much of the yard was taken up with an old structure: 'a freestanding maisonette of barge planking.' In this type of construction, piles were sunken into the ground with a sill placed upon them. After stud walls were erected, one-by-twelves, old planks from barges, were simply tacked up. 'Nails,' explains Dykes, 'were not galvanised, so that eventually the barge planks simply fell to the ground. Even so,' he adds, 'it took two years for the historical commission to tear it down.' The French Quarter is the oldest part of New Orleans. R. J. Dykes' house dates to about 1830, 'give or take five years.' Another remnant of his property's former life is an old well at one corner of a shady brick patio.

'It was basically a hole in the ground,' says Dykes, adding, 'some Tulane archaeology students dug it up and left me some of the bottles. I ended up using old bricks and building it up about 24 inches. It has clear water in it. I had it tested.' New Orleans, he explains, is below sea level. Even though the Quarter is the highest part of the city, one can observe the level of the ground water in the well. Right now, as registered in the well, water is about eight feet below the ground.

The ground water floats up other momentos of the city's past. When R. J. Dykes installed a pond four years ago, he took care to line the hole with 'layers and layers of newspaper and then roofing paper before laying down a layer of industrial plastic to hold the water. The soil is full of old pottery dishes and bits of clay pots.'

Today the pond water is barely visible for the wealth of water plants that it supports. There are tropical water lilies flowering, a white and a pink nightbloomer that stays open until nine the next morning. Pickerel weed blooms blue and water cabbage and water hyacinths compete for surface space. The water hyacinths multiply so rapidly that Dykes says 'once a week I throw them away.' Japanese koi and carp live in the pond as well.

A stone bridge crosses the pond. In a jungle of

vegetation around it are melon-coloured hibiscus, deep maroon zinnias, a thicket of ferns, and, between the paving stones, a ground cover of wild strawberry and mint. A pair of pink flamingos seem to gaze at their reflections in the water.

This part of the garden is alive with the calls and songs of birds. Just behind the pond is the old convent wall, on the other side of which are five great cedars. 'Doves, cardinals, and mocking birds nest in there,' says Dykes. His own purple martin house draws more birds into the garden. Of the house he jokes, 'you feel like you're the keeper of a timeshare – you have to clean up after them.' Each year he sees the first martins, 'the scouts,' during Mardi Gras. 'I don't know why,' he shrugs. 'They leave on the Fourth of July. They eat a lot of bugs. I love them.'

In summer, while the martins keep the insects under control, the garden is as full as it can be. Annuals bloom along with a parade of perennials. Along the side of the house, an angel trumpet datura, fifteen feet high, is covered with no fewer than one hundred flowers. Crinums bloom pink, white, and dark red above leathery foliage. The vegetable garden, dominated by the tall yellow flowers of Jerusalem artichokes, brings forth tomatoes, basil, and eggplant.

Autumn is to New Orleans gardeners what spring is to everyone else. By October, R. J. Dykes' crop of autumn snow peas is well under way. 'You have,' he explains, 'a whole vegetable-growing period before the freeze. Then around the first of February we can put in another.' Autumn also brings more blooms – even more datura flowers, the upright yellow blooms of the candelabra plant, and red cypress-vine flowers.

When winter finally arrives, the tropicals, orchids, bromeliads, frangipani, plumaria, palms, and cycads are moved inside a lean-to greenhouse on the far right, against the convent wall. Moving them in is a disagreeable chore. Dykes dislikes it, not only because 'it's such a

production,' but also because when the plants are gone, 'the whole yard becomes void.' If there is a freeze, another dismal prospect looms: the bananas have to be removed. Dykes says, 'they are an ugly, stinking mush mess that also stains your hands.'

However, even winter in New Orleans has its compensations: throughout December and January camellias bloom. All things considered, R. J. Dykes wouldn't garden anywhere else. Where else could one grow cycads, Japanese and American magnolias, day lilies, avocado, ginger and holly in one small garden? Where else is there a winter so gentle that every few years the bananas grow to two storeys? Where else are there 'usually six or seven or eight things blooming at any time of the year?' Even when the winter brings frost, the plants spring back at the first breath of spring. 'You can always count on the bananas to do twelve feet,' says R. J. Dykes, adding, 'that's New Orleans growth – you put in in and a month later it's all over the place.'

The lean-to conservatory is essential in R. J. Dykes' garden to provide shelter for the tender potted plants during winter months

133

THE HEBER-PERCYS

AQUARIANS

For anyone to claim that a particular swimming pool must be one of the most stylish in the world may imply that they have personally plunged in every pool from Acapulco to Palm Beach and from Positano to Peking. Well, he hasn't. But he is willing to do so, if he must, to support his claim about the pool at Faringdon House, Oxfordshire. The element of surprise, the homogeneity of the various parts, and the cool originality of the conception are such that to say 'there is nothing like it,' though banal, is merely to speak the truth.

One reason for its originality and its success is that the design of the pool bears no relation whatever to the style of its surroundings, and yet, instead of being alien to them, it adds another dimension to them.

The park in which the house sits was the site of an Elizabethan manor and the grounds – the conventional farmlands and fishponds – were turned into park and lake by the Poet Laureate, William Pye, in the early eighteenth century. His new house was splendidly situated with its front drive running past the church and park to the south, and its north front facing an uninterrupted plain of 30 miles or more to the Cotswolds beyond.

All the *Oxford Companion to Literature* says about Pye is that he was the constant butt of contemporary ridicule, but he did like a view, as we know from his only poem to survive in anthologies, about an air balloon, which goes:

Hail then ye daring few! who proudly soar
Through paths by mortal eye unviewed before!
. . . See earth's stupendous regions spread below,
    To hillocks shrunk the mountain's loftiest
    brow

Later, the house was looked after by the Cunard family and then in the 1930s by Lord Berners. In his day, it was the scene of fashionable house parties, 'Fridays to Mondays', where names to conjure with would include the Sitwells and Benjamin Britten. The present owner, Mr Robert Heber-Percy, therefore, is in possession of all the elements of the English country house: an approach by elegant raked gravel drive, past the walled and well-ordered kitchen garden, the orangery to the left, and, beyond, the elegant terrace, overlooking lawn and woodlands.

All the capabilities have been exploited. Mr Heber-Percy has kept up the house and park in the conventional way – by a vigorous programme of judicious tree-planting and good husbandry, and within such a framework there would be no necessity to do more.

However, one specific concept occupied Mr Heber-Percy's mind: a swimming pool. Some pool owners want theirs to be a conspicuous

The orangery and lily pool at Faringdon House where a Victorian military ancestor of the Heber-Percys seems rather smug about being inundated. It was the sort of joke that Robert Heber-Percy greatly enjoyed

feature of the garden; indeed, some will want it to be *the* conspicuous feature of their garden. There is one small house in fashionable Fulham, London, where the swimming pool occupies the entire garden. Space was not Mr Heber-Percy's problem, but Faringdon has a stylistic unity in which he felt a pool would be intrusive. He decided that the right course was to hide the pool from sight, not because it would be unsightly but because it could then be exactly as he wanted it – without concessions to the dominant English country-house style.

One obvious solution, and one which several owners of country houses have adopted, is to attempt to 'country-housify' the pool. This requires that the pool itself remain blue and tiled and chlorinated, but around it, as if to pretend it is not a pool, the owners have erected stone balustrades, stone urns, stone benches, and perhaps a statue or two of stone nymphs about to bathe. Other country house owners have gone further and hidden the pool in the recesses of a tall square of Leyland Cyprus or thick yew hedges.

Another solution, and one which may have briefly tempted Mr Heber-Percy, is to turn the orangery into an indoor pool. This is very commonly done, and the result is, in general, pretty, although it must be said that attempts to pretend that a pool was there in the orangery all the time, complete with urns and Chippendale wooden seats (from Chatsworth), strike a false note.

It did not suit Mr Heber-Percy to use the orangery, partly because he had a better idea, and partly because he finds the orangery extremely useful as a kind of garden-room extension to the house. Its walls are hung with several indifferent family portraits, and comfortable period furniture (but not of particular value) is strewn about among potted plants. He himself

admits that there are times when, if room has to be found for some piece of exotica for which no obvious home suggests itself, he will say, 'Put it in the orangery.' The atmosphere of the orangery, therefore, is a cross between a conservatory and a rather untidy study.

Outside the orangery, on an area of level ground about 40 metres square, is a large, shallow pond with a neat stone rim, and in the centre sits a stone bust, rather bleached, of one of Mr Heber-Percy's Victorian military ancestors. The gentleman concerned looks entirely satisfied to be occupying his pond, and the general impression is of a small cameo head in a picture frame. On the other side of this pond, opposite the orangery, is a tall bank about twelve feet high. Its dark ground-cover and shrubs contrast with the white and glass orangery, and the statue marooned in the pond stares straight ahead at the bank which can be climed by a series of wide, shallow stone steps. You climb, imagining that when you reach the last step there will be a distant vista of the park beyond. Instead, you stare out on to a 'medieval' swimming pool which could have been described by Sir Walter Scott. It is square and all in grey stone. At the left corner is a small stone turret with a conical roof. You might be standing in a medieval courtyard, although the centre of it is a pool – not a blue or green chlorinated pool, but a black, deep, mysterious-looking pool from whose depths a hand clutching Excalibur might at any moment appear.

Ahead, in the centre of the containing wall on the far side of the pool, are two huge stone wyverns. These are of the genus 'Queen's Beasts', heraldic animals first sculpted for Queen Elizabeth, and this particular pair, date of birth unknown, were obtained in Cornwall by Mr Heber-Percy. 'They breed in Cornwall, you know,' he says. The wyverns appear to be guarding the pool, in a friendly way, and a pair of

Intimidating heraldic wyverns might prevent the faint-hearted from entering the mysterious dark waters of the medieval courtyard swimming pool at Faringdon House

137

Italianate wooden chairs by the side of the pool also have an animal motif.

Style is not so much a matter of having a brilliant conception, but of carrying it through with meticulous attention to detail. Mr Heber-Percy's detail includes an interesting floor surface in the turret-tower, created by sinking hundreds of old pennies in a symmetrical pattern. The colour of the pool's inside surface is another meticulously thought out feature – this was achieved by mixing special dyes with the cement during construction.

Much might be said about the gardens and park around Faringdon House. Mr Heber-Percy has sensitively maintained the general design developed by those who lived in the house in earlier centuries. It is true that he has introduced certain eccentric touches such as the doves that he has dyed in many colours to adorn the drive and lawn. But the pool is not eccentric – in relation to the park it is a small gem which sets off the park, similar in its way to the Picasso which the present owner has hung among the more classical portraits in the entrance hall at Faringdon.

Sharing some genes with his uncle Robert, it is not surprising that on the other side of England Algernon Heber-Percy has also become a fine gardener. His garden at Hodnet Hall near Market Drayton in Shropshire has long featured in the itinerary of important garden visits. Its main attraction has always been, and is likely to remain, a spectacularly lovely water garden comprising a chain of stepped lakes created by damming a lake in nine places. This forms the spine of the garden and was built by Algernon Heber-Percy's father, beginning in 1922. And since by then the era of grand gardening was more or less at an end in England, it was indeed a very stylish flourish which ultimately turned what had been merely a marshy hollow with its

banks a mass of elders, laurels and rushes, into an outstanding show garden. With their lime-free soil, the banks of the lakes have favoured the establishment of notable plantings of azaleas, rhododendrons, camellias and ericaceous plants, which flourish under acid conditions.

As well as supporting the normal aquatic plants, the edges of the streams and pools in the garden are ideal for the candelabra primulas, irises and bog plants which are a special feature at Hodnet.

The late Brigadier Heber-Percy's work at Hodnet hung a fine skirt of garden on to the large Elizabethan-style south-facing hall which was built in 1870 on a plateau above the largest lake. Algernon and Lady Heber-Percy, who are now responsible for the gardens, continue to enrich the lake banks and the immediate surrounds of the house by judicious planting which is especially designed to increase the interest of the garden during the weeks between April and October when it is open to the public. Like the Brigadier, they too carefully foster the interests of a bevy of velvety black swans and the many other species of ornamental waterfowl which add distinctly romantic animation to the landscape.

Recently, however, they felt obliged to modernise and reduce the size of the house to make it easier to manage. The main changes which they made included removing the top floor and replacing the roof and permanently removing the roof of one wing on the northern side of the house.

If the wing had been completely demolished, the whole balance of the north façade would have been upset. So the Heber-Percys decided to leave two of the walls intact, taking out the southern and western walls to allow full access to the sun. When the remaining walls had been reinforced, all demolition scars on their inner surfaces were hidden beneath a smooth rendering of cement. The result was a perfectly pro-

138

Tasteful paving and architectural trelliswork were used to transform an abandoned wing of Hodnet Hall into a wonderfully sheltered area of garden

tected growing area which the Heber-Percys have exploited beautifully to create a small formal garden which, in its style, isolation and confinement, contrasts splendidly with the sweeping landscapes of the rest of the garden.

The large, plain internal surfaces have been lined with highly decorative trellis panels. The ground has been covered with large round cobbles in one-metre rectangles separated by lines of terracotta tiles. This provides hard standing for a central stone basin planted with a tall fuchsia flanked by geraniums and *Senecio maritima*, and for tubs of lilies and rhododendrons such as *R. 'Wilbrit'* and *R. 'Pink Sensation'*. Two large mounds of lavender are planted into the pavement at the feet of a pair of espaliered *Magnolia grandiflora* on the west-facing wall.

A tight row of *Hydrangea serrata* 'Grayswood' form a plant 'seat' below the stone mullions of what was the north window, and a *Hydrangea petiolaris* clambers up its flanking wall. From this walled enclosure visitors can look down into an area of smooth lawn surrounded by tightly clipped yew which forms chunky, dark-green walls to screen a simple Roman-apsed swimming pool with no distracting embellishments – a triumph of understatement.

In the gravel which fronts the northern façade of the house, to make an attractive turning point for cars, there is a delightful water feature. Water from a simple fountain at the top of a wedding cake arrangement spills over three tiers of shallow stone basins of increasing diameter supported by old straddle stones. The fountain is set centrally in a much larger dry basin planted with glowing yellow 'Coronet' antirrhinums.

The garden at Hodnet Hall which is 5½ miles south west of Market Drayton in Shropshire is open between 1st April and 30th September.

THE BERWINDS

ANIMAL CRACKERS

Seen from across a large stretch of svelte lawn with its rose-pink and light grey stucco walls and pedimented and pilastered portico, Graham and Sigrid Berwind's house at Bryn Mawr seems to be a typical noble Philadelphia 'Main-Line' home. But if the sun makes the beautifully proportioned windows twinkle like amused eyes it could be because the Berwinds have surrounded it with a delicate blend of elegance and whimsy. Not so *outré* as blatantly to defy snooty Bryn Mawr gardening conventions, with subtlety the Berwinds have carried through an exciting adventure in garden style. And, like all talented designers, they were aware from the beginning of the need for a garden to be appropriate to its site.

In the Philadelphia garden the mood is one of polished urbanity: at their summer home on Mount Desert Island off the northern coast of Maine, all is delicately manipulated wilderness.

Originally the Bryn Mawr property offered a predictably flat and large rectangular plot of scant interest. But, using their discreet magic, the Berwinds have transformed it into a series of smoothly integrated but quite distinct environments. Differences in colour and ambience are produced by careful selection of varieties and the thoughtful introduction of well-sited individual specimen plants which stamp their character on the surrounding area. Unity has been imposed on the whole scheme thanks to the Berwinds' impeccable sense of horticultural harmony and their courage in creating not just flowerbeds but whole communities of sympathetically associated plants.

Although such skills are rare, there is nothing startlingly unconventional about that. However, the Berwinds are adept at concealing their gardening tricks – clutching their plans and catalogues tight to their chests. The illusion of serene normality is amplified by a truly grand, and almost *de rigueur*, English-style herbaceous border which is all pinks and lavenders, blues and silvers, and which is designed to bloom in spring and autumn.

A pair of handsome, erect camellias flank the front door like a brace of confidently deferential major domos, but at the feet of the camellias, below the sight line of their blossoms, the Berwinds have stationed savage beasts: not familiar eighteenth-century lions *couchant* or heraldic-looking leopards, but a pair of African savannah killers – splendid bronze models of a grumbling hippo and an angry rhinoceros. Fleeing from them, visitors would find no sanctuary in the more heavily wooded area of the garden because, lurking dangerously, half-concealed in a mattress of ground-covering ivy, is a full-sized bronze crocodile with jaws gaping greedily to receive them.

It's not often that garden strollers are likely to encounter this sort of surprise

There's nothing namby-pamby or anthropomorphic about the sculpture with which the Berwinds have embellished their Bryn Mawr garden. Don't be deceived by the apparent docility of this hippo – he's a true African killer

Right: *Jumbo at lunch –
a reminder of a happy
holiday in India*

Far right: *The ghautama
at repose among the
Bryn Mawr foliage and
flowers prompts
recollections of the
mystic East*

142

Apart from satisfying the Berwinds' penchant for fine animal sculpture, these tongue-in-cheek terrors were sited to provide a shocking contrast to the idyll of a fine and only mildly curious Marini horse peering placidly across the lawn from his hock-deep station in a bold band of pachysandra pasture established to give him year-round grazing.

Neither is there anything too threatening about the bronze Indian elephant emerging from a tangle of tall rhododendrons in another part of the garden. He could be taking his lunch break at a logging camp high in the Himalayas. And to come across him, half-revealed, as one comes across the bronze birds and the stone-carved Buddha from Bali in other sites, adds up to a string of gentle and utterly pleasing surprises.

For the Berwinds, the sculptures are more than mere ornaments; they provoke memories of other places loved or admired. Japan is recalled in a simple, abstract dark bronze sculpture mounted on an elegant yoke of lighter-coloured carved stone and set amongst gracefully pruned cut-leaf maples. The softly needled paths which wind beneath the canopy of mature white pine

and eastern hemlock among a thick underplanting of hostas, astilbes and ferns, and the rough stone basins which collect rainwater and reflect passing clouds, are redolent of summers in Maine. A paved terrace with a formal octagonal pool, precisely cut stone coping and the splendid terracotta oil jar beyond evoke fond memories of scorching days in Rome. A vista along stepping stones in grass leading deep into a wood offers glimpses of a simple plumed fountain tumbling languidly back into a lily pond and the spiky head of a cordyline palm summons up images of Moorish gardens in Seville.

It is the perfect positioning of their artefacts which best demonstrates the Berwinds' mastery of design. The solo position of a large bronze Chinese pot inlaid with coloured enamel on a broad carpet of tightly-clipped lawn permits the beauty of its elegantly simple lines to be fully appreciated. The smooth terracotta of the oil jar near the Roman pool glows in fine contrast to the dark rough bark of the trunk of the tree at whose feet it stands. A trio of smoothly rounded stones is grouped with unerring good taste to embellish the surround of the octagonal pool.

The Berwinds' Marini horse has been given a rich pasture of **Pachysandra** *to graze*

Reflections in the water in a stone basin at Bryn Mawr evoke memories of woodland pools in the Berwinds' other garden on the coast of Maine

Abstract sculpture of this type is always enjoyed the most when cleverly sited in a garden where it is enhanced by the changing shadow play of foliage and can benefit from the textural contrasts highlighted there

144

Apart from their evocation of the Mediterranean, classical terracotta Ali Baba jars like the one shown here make wonderful beckoning features in gardens

Paving stones have been omitted from areas of a small, sunny courtyard beside the kitchen to leave room for herbs and treasured vegetables, but frugality and utility are not allowed to dominate. A gigantic, full-bellied, earthenware oil jar – cracked, but acquired for the beauty of its shape alone – looms in one corner. And shrubs in simple but pleasing large clay nursery pots are scattered with studied abandon, enhancing the decoration with their foliage and flowers.

The way in which the Berwinds have deliberately had the pointing of an old stone boundary wall heavily emphasised by specifying a very light-coloured grout thickly applied is audacious and clearly demonstrates their ability to manage detail to great effect.

Their confident touch has extended to the way in which they handle plants. A thick grove of white-stemmed birch makes an unusual feature in the Philadelphia region, their trunks contrasting wonderfully with a low, dark, evergreen undergrowth through which packed white narcissi push in spring. Very large, clean-edged swatches of evergreen ground-cover – notably of pachysandra and creeping juniper – characterise the bold planting which the Berwinds favour. Even in mid-winter they ensure that the garden surface is excitingly patterned. But this preoccupation with the large effect hasn't distracted them from the need to provide whimsical touches such as neat clumps of grape hyacinths for the hippo to gobble.

The Berwinds planned their Maine garden as the perfect complement to their Bryn Mawr property. There is no lawn: its role has been ceded to velvety mosses, blueberry, winter-green and bunchberry sods. It is a naturally varied landscape situated atop pink and grey granite ledges with a sweeping view down the length of the Somes Sound, the only true fjord on the east coast of the USA. With many of its native ecol-

At their summer home in Maine the Berwinds have only tinkered with nature minimally to produce a stylish natural woodland garden

ogical niches intact, it required the most delicate of touches to create a garden which would not seem ludicrously competitive in such grand surroundings.

Their main intervention, apart from mowing paths through the property, is an initimate crescent of uncommon annuals and midsummer-blooming perennials on the edge of the woods. Low granite benches complete the circle, providing fine seating from which to admire their favourite cool blues, lavenders, pinks, silvers, and whites in the border, which contrast so beautifully with the duns and duller greens of the natural woodlands.

Notable among the perennials in the crescent are silver-leafed artemesias, numerous varieties of astilbes, many campanulas both large and small (including *C. carpatica*, *C. garganica major*, *C. lactiflora* and *C. pulla*), *Clematis tangutica*, blue delphiniums, foxgloves, dicentras, hardy geraniums, hostas, many varieties of lily, and the smaller phlox and common mallows.

All are plants which are capable of enduring bleak winters and which tolerate salt-laden gales. These are further enriched by many annuals, including blue and pink salvias, scabious, snapdragons, anchusas, nicotianas and cosmos — nothing too sophisticated which might hint at a suburban garden.

A newly completed project takes advantage of a natural granite outcropping as a backdrop for a trickle of water which feeds a tiny woodland pool that they have excavated.

The Berwinds felt no compulsion to change any feature of a natural lichen garden jutting out beyond a sandy cove within the view of a favoured bald eagle's perch. Confronted there by shy ospreys and loons, squabbling gulls and the surge of the tide, they were obliged to conclude that, when on form, Nature is the most stylish designer of all, and there are few better places in the world to see her at her most awe-inspiring than on the rugged coast of Maine.

Zandra Rhodes

DREAMS METROPOLITAN

Zandra Rhodes has a strong visual sense and a powerful personality and it is no surprise that both her office and her house closely reflect her concept of what design is about. Perhaps it should come as no surprise that her sense of style is carried through quite so uncompromisingly into her garden, but the fact is that Zandra Rhodes, her office and house, her fashion business and her garden are all of one piece.

She admits that fifteen years ago she knew nothing about gardening, had never grown a single plant 'except the plastic variety'. What changed all that was a comment made by a decorator who was helping her with the transformation of the large Victorian terrace house she had bought in the Notting Hill Gate area of London. 'You had better do something about the garden,' he said. It was an exaggeration, in those days, to call it a garden. A tiny area, north facing, with practically no sunlight, and very high walls, perhaps twenty feet up on all three sides. Like many London back gardens, it is at basement level. There was even an outside loo, presumably for the use of the Victorian domestics as the area was too small to have needed the services of a gardener.

The first idea was to cover the walls (and such other parts as would not resent it) with green growth, beginning with a Russian vine. It was at this stage that a friend presented Zandra Rhodes with an eight-foot-long replica of a kind of Mexican god in a reclining pose, made in polystyrene and probably originally constructed for commercial display. This sparked off a new notion of the garden. 'He', the Mexican god, had to be given a place in it worthy of 'His' status, and so a series of steps was built up from ground level, using glass mirror bricks on many of the horizontal surfaces. He was placed slightly above eye level, lying on a kind of altar. In a sense, the garden as it is today was built around Him although He is by no means an over-dominant feature – merely part of the scenery.

Zandra Rhodes also decided at this stage that the garden, small as it was, should become a major feature of the house, and she re-designed her dressing room, also down at basement level, so that it became a kind of conservatory with sliding doors giving onto the garden. The room is full of indoor plants which melt into the rather wilder fantasy out of doors. Similarly, she altered the window of her bedroom, which also overlooks the garden, so that from there she has the full benefit of all the greenery beyond. Finally, she let the garden take over the roof terrace above the dressing room, which is big enough to sit out on, and which also overlooks the garden area below.

By virtue of these changes, the garden became

part of the design of the house, an inside-outside synthesis, or perhaps 'synergy' would be a better word, because garden and house interacted with each other as Zandra Rhodes imprinted on the outside the same passion for pattern and colour which was already in full possession inside the house.

The structure of the garden – the three high brick walls with the steps climbing up the far one – shaped the overall style, which is continued on the overlooking terrace and in the conservatory which links the garden area and the house at ground level. Zandra Rhodes has chosen mainly white flowers and foliage which is tolerant of shade. In the first category are *Hydrangea petiolaris*, hellebores, foxgloves, hart's-tongue, Solomon's seal, hostas and pachysandra. All are grown in pots as there is virtually no soil in the tiny basement area. Some of these plants are placed up the steps alongside bamboo grasses, and azaleas. Falling down from the top of the wall is the original russian vine and, climbing up another, an unusual red-leaved vine.

There is no doubt that, had Zandra Rhodes lived in the last century, she would have been one of the Ladies of the Camellias. She admits to being 'hooked on camellias'. The varieties she has chosen flower from early February and continue through to the summer. These include *C. X williamsii* 'Donation', and 'Citation', *C. japonica alba plena*, and C. reticulata. Grown, like everything else, in pots, the camellias receive special loving attention, being watered every other day. 'You feed them blood and talk to them,' says Zandra when pressed about her success with the camellias.

The mirrors on the steps reflect this greenery and add to the temple-like atmosphere created by the slumbering god; and yet there is an informality about it all – the Mexican god has a hosta on his belly and an aralia on his feet. Zandra Rhodes has fixed to the walls a number of long, flat coloured slabs, pilasters which support nothing, and which hint at the presence of a forgotten civilisation amongst the foliage. Here and there, climbing up the walls, are pieces of mirror in an irregular pattern, like glass plants, or, more probably, waterfalls momentarily caught and transfixed.

It is most reminiscent of the ruins of an ancient religious site suddenly discovered by explorers in the heart of the jungle, but the impression that one has been transported to foreign parts from Notting Hill Gate is soon dispelled by the presence of such homely items as chimney pots (holding hostas), roses, ivy, ferns and an easily recognised hydrangea. There is pottery everywhere, which Zandra Rhodes places with no particular concern for symmetry or straight lines. Apart from the walls and the steps, there are no straight lines.

The inside-outside conservatory area is filled with more tender plants, including a huge hanging plant with a marked resemblance to moose horns. These are nurtured by overhead 'sun

147

With his libation of potted plants, the abiding deity reclines on his mirror-fronted dais to dominate Zandra Rhodes' backyard garden

Oriental carved-wood pilasters relieve the monotony of Zandra Rhodes' backyard wall

148

lamps'. The exotic style of the garden beyond is carried through by such clever touches as a vast bowl of brown nutshells. Some of the outside plants, such as the Christmas cactus, are brought in here during the winter and Zandra covers others with insulating polythene bubble-sheets.

Above the conservatory is the terrace area. Here there is a wider variety of potted plants, more camellias and a large *Magnolia stellata*. This is Zandra Rhodes' kitchen garden, where she specialises in a variety of herbs and some interesting currant bushes all grown in pots or tubs.

So much for the back of the house. The front entrance also reflects Zandra Rhodes' individual taste. There is one of those small basement areas from which rises a magnificent russian vine, but, unlike most russian vines in London, this one has not been allowed to develop with wild abandon. 'When visiting China,' she explains, 'I learnt how to control the growth of plants by speaking to them and explaining what I wanted.' By this method (and the employment of a little wire and string) she persuaded the vine to go along the front railings, up the walls and along the balconies in regular festoons. The effect here is much more 'stagey' than at the back, accentuated by the strong classical lines of the house. The formality is offset by a balcony of roses and, near the front door, a giant hydrangea and cork screw stemmed hazel.

Just as her work is distinctly her own, so Zandra Rhodes' garden is unmistakably her own too. Yet there are lessons here for everyone: boldness, contrast, and a will to encourage plants to flourish in an environment far removed from the habitat to which they are normally accustomed have brought about marvellous results. Perhaps the supreme lesson is that even a very small and unpromising space – little more than a shady yard – can be made into a pleasing and exciting garden by the exercise of personal style.

EMBLEMATIC

151

*Hardly anything in an
emblematic garden is as
straightforward as it
seems. Many of the
artefacts and plants are
used as metaphors for
something else*

FULCHER, CARTER AND TATE

NEW FORMS, OLD INSPIRATIONS

At its most basic, gardening involves the arrangement of forms and colours in space. And, as such, it is as much the province of sculptors as carving a lump of rock and placing it on a plinth. This, at least, is the strongly held belief of sculptors George Carter, Raf Fulcher and Elizabeth Tate who, together with horticulturist Caroline Boisset, created what many people felt was the most interesting exhibit at the 1985 Chelsea Flower Show.

Their offering – the smallest garden layout at Chelsea – was called, with tongue in cheek, 'A Vision of Versailles', and it displayed more style and provoked more comment than anything which had appeared at Chelsea for years. In reinterpreting the grand manner and quiet charm of a seventeenth-century formal garden to fit the requirements of town gardeners, in their own words they made 'a deliberate attempt to break away from current garden style, in which the layout is characterised by uneasy curves and lack of symmetry and a complicated palette of plant material.'

Four dark, heavily rusticated pillars marked the entrance to a central and two side alleys which were separated from each other by high 'walls' of dark trellis framework inside which grew yew hedges. These alleys were given the illusion of greater length by subtly diminishing the size of their elements the further they were located from the viewpoint.

The central alley ended in a grotto constructed of blocks of stone, mirror glass and shell, embellished with moss and ferns. While the dark pillars, trellis framework and yew produced a mood of sombre mystery, this was immediately dispelled by the glitter of the grotto and the sparkle of light reflected from a series of silvered glass spheres ranged down the centre of the alley. Mounted on slim 'stalks', they could have been interpreted as notional allium flowers, or even 'Seers' orbs' or cyclopean eyes.

To mirror the sky and reflect more light around the dark framework of the central alley, a thin film of water was confined to one area of the stone paving. These reflections could be animated by gently revolving part of the bottom of the shallow 'pool'.

Small topiary specimens in simple geometric shapes – cones, balls and pyramids – formed from box and yew were used to embellish the two side alleys, which culminated in glass panels backed with metallic foil to reflect the light.

To increase the variety of experience offered in such a small space, there was a cross vista through a pedimented gateway into a short alley which pierced all the trellis walls. Small box-edged beds and knots near the entrances to the main alleys and at the foot of the trellis contained santolina, hyssop, rue, *Festuca glauca*, *Alchemilla mollis*, white lily-flowered tulips and forget-me-nots and conformed to a restrained blue, green, grey and white theme. Elsewhere, pots and containers held violets, *Rhamnus alaterna angustifolia* and cornflowers.

No matter whether they liked or loathed this garden, few people who saw it could deny that it was imbued with a wonderful sense of style.

But what were three sculptors doing at the Chelsea Flower Show? According to Raf Fulcher, garden design is the logical extension of sculpture: 'In the 1960s sculpture got down off the plinth and started to spread about the floor, and once it had been demonstrated that sculpture had no margins, there was nothing to stop it flowing out of doors or, for that matter, the whole garden being considered as a sculpture. After all, in many respects, garden designers and sculptors, or indeed painters, have similar concerns. They are all interested in using space and in how light changes affect their forms and colours. And gardens, just as much as other forms of art, have always reflected man's view of nature.'

Raf Fulcher feels that gardening has lost some of those exciting qualities which were commonplace in the seventeenth century when gardens were considered to be more than merely pretty adjuncts to houses. 'Then they weren't afraid to consider them as outside rooms designed to prompt contemplation. But all that was swept away by the landscape movement in the eighteenth century and the excitement of accelerating plant introductions of the nineteenth century which led to "Chocolate Box" gardening in which design was considered less important than creating a jumbled mass of colour.'

This is a tradition which Fulcher feels still dominates gardening today. And he isn't very impressed by those rare attempts to change direction which he has seen. 'Most gardens are small and closely related to small houses and it's no good pretending that they can be landscaped like parkland or made to resemble wild moorland, because such features can never be miniaturised convincingly.' He does, however, feel that formal gardens can be very satisfying even when recreated on a modest scale. Such artefacts as the small-scaled reconstituted-stone 'topiary' – obelisks, pyramids, spheres – with which his collaborator George Carter won a prize in the *Sunday Times* 'Art for the Garden' competition at the International Festival of the Garden at Liverpool in 1984, help to make small-scale formality really satisfying, Fulcher feels.

To the accusation that, because so much of it was dark, their Chelsea garden was melancholic, its creators reply that melancholia is not the same as misery: 'It merely means a mood which is thoughtful or contemplative. Why shouldn't

The heavily rusticated entrance to the cross alley in the 'Vision of Versailles' garden at the 1985 Chelsea Flower Show. The whole scene can be animated by disturbing the reflections in the surface of the shallow central pool; this is done by spinning the knob which in turn causes a section of the floor to revolve

153

thoughts be happy as well as sad?' Fulcher asks.

The ability to make people look twice, and to think – and smile – is an essential ingredient in style, Elizabeth Tate believes: 'Nothing could be considered to have style which hasn't got such a commanding presence and elegance that it compels further examination. Or else a certain awkwardness which prevents it from being merely *chichi*. A really stylish object or place will make you look several times before you grasp its full significance. And it would be bound to have wit: because you can't have style without lightness of touch and great exuberance.'

Asked to nominate the most stylish garden features they have seen, Fulcher and Tate chose the terraces at Rieuvaulx Abbey in Yorkshire and at St Germain en Laye near Paris, and the round pool and basilica lawn at Hidcote in Gloucestershire. Modesty clearly forbade them from mentioning their achievements in their own garden at Wrekenton in County Durham; their work with George Carter, which was such a notable feature of the 1986 Garden Festival at Stoke-on-Trent; or the fine allegorical garden which this talented trio created for the Chelsea Flower Show in 1987.

RAF FULCHER GARDEN PLAN:
Eighton Cottage

A Gravel drive
B House
C Lawn
D1 Timber boarded parterres. 'Roses: violets: pinks'
D2 Timber boarded parterres. 'Roses: primroses: autumn crocus'

1 Rock grotto
2 Pool: white water lily
3 Clipped hawthorns
4 Clipped box
5 6'0" stone wall
6 Ash tree
7 Wild flowers
8 Mint; wild cyclamen
9 Burnet rose
10 Mixed border

11 Stone retaining wall
12 Sycamore tree
13 Lilacs
14 Viburnum dunwoodii
15 7'0" stone wall
16 Climber rose
17 Small 18" stone obelisks
18 Planted urn
19 Viburnum opulus; Winter jasmine
20 5'0" stone wall

21 Hawthorn
22 Stone recess
23 Hawthorn
24 Grass bank
25 Ash tree
26 Old roses in wooden trellis obelisks
27 Lavender hedges
28 Box cones in cases
29 Ash tree: mature
30 Timber fences

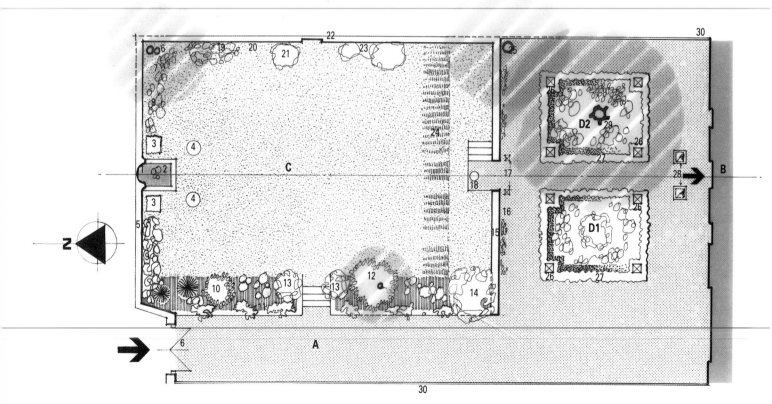

RAF FULCHER: Eighton Cottage

A Entrance drive: gravel
B Stone grotto
C Lawn
D1 Timber boarded parterres.
[Roses; violets; pinks]
D2 Timber boarded parterres.
[Roses; primroses; autumn crocus]

1 Pool
2 Hawthorn pillars
3 6'0" stone wall
4 Ash and 6 sycamore
5 5'0" stone wall
7 Helleborus Niger William; cottage
poppies; ox eye daisies; delphiniums
8 Laurel; Viburnum burkwoodii;
primroses and cowslips
9 7'0" stone wall
10 Climbing roses
11 and 12 Mature ash trees
13 Lavender hedges
14 Trellis obelisks with old roses
15 Box cones in cases
16 Boarded fence

*An attractive small
mount and obelisk made
by George Carter*

At Wrekenton, Fulcher and Tate have demonstrated convincingly how a garden rich in fantasy can be created to embellish a relatively small plot skirting a modest, if charming, home. The house is fronted by an 80 foot by 25 foot rectangle of land subdivided by a cross wall a third of the way down the plot. A central alley from the door of the house penetrates the dividing wall, providing a long view to an alcove grotto at the far end of the garden. The first third of the alley is gravelled. The implied walkway beyond the dividing wall is of raised lawn with conically clipped box growing in containers to define the track.

For a few minutes each day sunlight is reflected back along the central axis from a mirror in the grotto, through the front door, to light a statue in the hall. Immediately outside the door, semi-formal low beds, *parterre* hedged by

The vista to the mirror grotto down the central axis of the Wrekenton garden

low clipped box and set in gravel, surround trellis obelisks with fragrant pillar roses.

At Stoke-on-Trent, Fulcher and Carter used timber and painted hessian to create large-scale, cheap 'Renaissance' structures such as archways, haystack gazebos and obelisks. These surrounded and provided a backing for a large grass amphitheatre of the type which was used for entertainments in large gardens in the seventeenth and eighteenth centuries. Elizabeth Tate carved charming interpretations of heraldic beasts in wood and mounted them on colourful wooden pillars to line and enliven the walkway in the formal garden.

The trio's main concern at Chelsea in 1987 was the way in which our perception of garden structures and plants changes with alterations in the quality and intensity of light. They used box trellising, infilled with hedging plants, and other wooden structures to divide the plot by two diagonal alleys. One alley stressed the clarity and optimism of the day; the other the mystery and pessimism of the night. A grotto at the end of the dark alley could be more or less obscured by moving a series of hinged screens fixed at the alley margins. Altering the position of the screen was done by hand.

At the intersection they located an intriguing hydraulic/pneumatic fountain crowned with a large gilded copper sphere from which four water jets emerged. In essence (see drawing and explanation) the fountain was inspired by Raf Fulcher's studies of the seventeenth-century work of Isaac de Causse, a Swiss grotto builder and hydraulic engineer, and Thomas Bushell, whose extremely complicated and imaginative waterworks in a garden in Oxfordshire became known as the 'Enstone Marvels'. By their understanding of simple hydraulic and pneumatic principles they both successfully provided answers to the question: 'How do you eject water above the height of its source?' It was the sort of problem which intrigued natural philsophers in an era when the frontiers between the arts and sciences were blurred.

Fulcher's large, shining sphere fountain surrounded by satellites of spherical clipped bay trees – an obvious and attractive emblem of the sun, the source of all life – would, he hoped, spark off some fruitful melancholy. But why, he was asked, when clearly de Causse and Bushell would have rejoiced in the natural phenomenon of electricity, didn't he rely on a simple submerged electric pump to push the water up from the underground reservoir to his sphere, or for that matter to power the fountain jets? Why did he rely on a hand-pump (of the type which used

The pneumatic/ hydraulic fountain in the Fulcher, Carter and Tate garden at the 1987 Chelsea Flower Show as seen when looking along the diagonal pathway representing darkness or night

157

**CARTER, FULCHER, TATE
ALLEGORICAL GARDEN:**
Chelsea '86

A:B Morning to afternoon AXIS
C:D Dusk to night AXIS
E Symbolic carved elm head sculpture 'SUMMER'
F Symbolic carved elm head sculpture 'WINTER'
G Copper sphere 'SUN' fountain feature

1 Raised pools
2 Pump for fountain

3 Facing kiosks
4 and 5 Housing for armillary sphere and stage flats
6 Pyramidical roof
7 Tall pyramidical trellis: enclosing yew – dark
8 Tall pyramidical trellis: enclosing hawthorn – light
9 Strip planting: dark colours
10 Strip planting: light colours
11 Hessian-backed timber trellis
12 Open timber trellis
13 Split chestnut screens
14 Raised planting beds

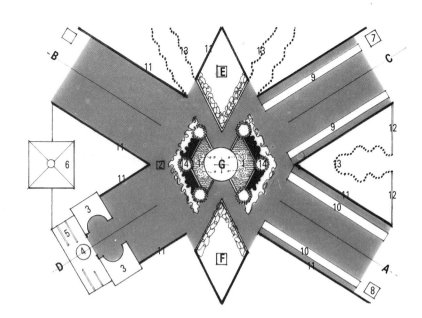

158

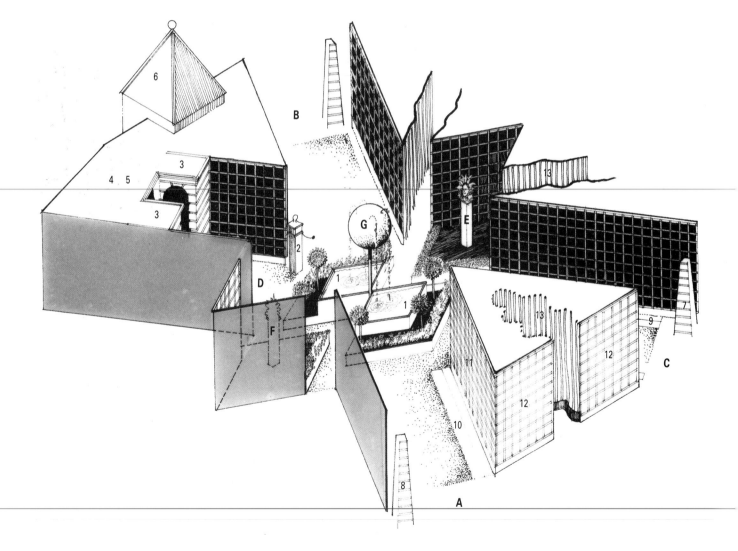

to be commonplace on every village green)? 'Because,' he answered, 'throwing a switch has become such an unthinking act that it wouldn't provoke a moment's contemplation. But if gardeners are obliged to do the pumping for five minutes and sweat a bit, when they sit back to rest for twenty minutes and watch the jets cascading, it might make them think about what they have actually been doing and how they have harnessed natural phenomena to create an attractive effect; and once they begin to ponder questions like that, goodness knows where their imaginations might take them. But it is certain that for a while they won't be preoccupied with more mundane matters and that should give them the sort of mental repose which all good gardens are supposed to offer.'

Close-up of the fountain sphere showing its four jets

CARTER, FULCHER, TATE ALLEGORICAL GARDEN, CHELSEA '86: Fountain Section and Function

(1) On/Off valve in open position, allows water falling into raised pools (2) from fine water jets in 'golden sphere' (3) to drain into underground collecting cistern (4) which in turn compresses the air, forcing it up through pipe (5) putting pressure on the surface of the water inside the sphere (6) This forces the water through the siphon pipes and the fine jets.

TO REFILL: When the sphere is empty, it is refilled by closing the On/Off valve (1) and operating the hand pump (7) for successful operation the cistern (4) should be located further below ground level than the jets in the sphere are located above it.

Ryan Gainey

MEMORIES

Ryan Gainey is a passionate, sensitive gardener. He is also an avid collector. Above all, he is an *arranger* of his great collection. Over the years, he has amassed plants, garden art, and impressions from the gardens he has worked on, visited, remembered. His romantic, eclectic garden style has come together only after a lifetime of accumulating and gathering plants – 'from ditch banks, deserted country yards, gardening friends throughout the world' – and, above all, memories from every garden he has ever seen.

When he began the garden seven years ago, Mr Gainey admits that he was 'burning with passion to grow and plant. Initially, there was more desire than knowledge, so lots of plants have been composted and now have been replanted with more understanding about the use of plants. I was as ignorant as most people, but one must begin to learn any form of self-expression. So I just started planting lots of annuals.'

Later, 'having acquired a bit of patience and humility,' he began to garden thoughtfully, with 'more quiet knowledge.' He then set about creating 'a rustic, nostalgic cottage garden, which has prevailed through all these years of learning.'

The first of four entrances to the garden opens onto a straight stone path which bisects the newest section of garden on recently acquired property. Beds here support vegetables, a wealth of poppies in spring and, later, annuals. The path leads to a brick-walled vegetable and herb garden – also new and created in homage to the lovely vegetable and herb garden at Barnsley, designed by Rosemary Verey, for whom Mr Gainey expresses great fondness and admiration. The space within the walls is divided into four quadrants. In each section a standard rose is encircled by bright green lettuces. Pink dianthus, boxwood and lavender form diamond patterns with the patterns of the walks.

Another entrance to the garden from the street is a central gate that opens onto a path of broad stone rectangles. Once, these stones served as coping for raised flower beds when the property supported the city's very first wholesale cut-flower business. On both sides the path is edged by a mixed border in the best English tradition. So perfect is the likeness, with tall spires of delphinium and larkspur, that the garden could serve as the model for a picture postcard from the Cotswolds. It takes a while for the realisation to sink in: the garden is a counterfeit. Delphiniums do not survive Georgia's long tropical summers. Nor do English daisies, tulips, centaurias, or forget-me-nots. Most are as foreign to the intense heat of the Georgia summer as ferns to the Sahara. Enormous love, labour,

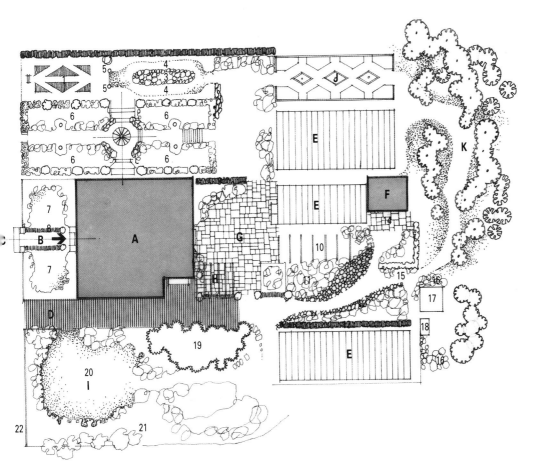

161

and a little bit of madness are required to sustain this glorious illusion.

Each year, Mr Gainey buys 4″ liners of delphiniums from a grower. These are set out in the garden in January or February. Then all the rest is treated as annuals and planted in November. Each year new plants luxuriate for a few weeks in the soft warmth of the Georgia spring before they succumb to the blistering summer heat and are taken out in July.

A well developed collection of clipped and unclipped evergreens for structure and herbaceous plants and flowering shrubs for colour and interest holds the border together. Evergreens are especially important because the growing season is so long.

'We in the South,' explains Mr Gainey, 'have both a spring . . . *and* a summer crop.' Dependable flowering shrubs – spireas, viburnums, althea, hydrangeas – begin in January and continue until summer. In addition, Japanese, German, and Siberian iris, anemones, *Aster tatarica*, *Coreopsis verticillata*, *Boltonia*, and phlox can be counted on to bloom over the summer. 'Mt. Fuji', a white phlox, will even bloom twice if deadheaded.

Midway down the border, the path circles around a spring bed of forget-me-nots. Here, a white wrought-iron Victorian settee serves as focal point for a side path that connects the first garden with the perennial border. Ryan Gainey turned bad luck into good fortune when an unusual frost killed large crepe myrtles some years ago. He fashioned the trunks with their exfoliating bark into a pergola that now shelters the bench.

162

Above: Called a 'gazing ball', this ceramic piece was once the pride of a southern garden

*Far right:
Under a pergola fashioned from the trunks of crepe myrtles, a white wrought-iron settee looks over a spring planting of forget-me-nots. The paving stones were once used as coping for flower beds when the property was a cut-flower nursery*

from having to have air conditioning.' The rustic settee is a new reproduction Mr Gainey commissioned. The original was the first cast-iron bench made in America. Originals were used at the Crystal Palace in England.

Next to the house a driveway leads past this side garden, culminating in an outdoor living area. Here, the functions and comforts of the house spill out over a covered porch down a short flight of steps to a stone patio. On the porch is Mr Gainey's bathroom, an addition to an old house that predated indoor plumbing, from which a large window overlooks the patio. Its location makes a long, leisurely bath seem like a dip in a tropical pool surrounded by greenery.

The patio is a transitional space. It is a place where the comforts of the inside mingle with garden elements brought closer by means of pots and containers. In the mild Georgia climate, living out of doors is pleasant for at least half of the year.

Pieces of Alabama swamp-willow furniture – a settee positioned under a grapevine-covered arbour that is hung with bells, and a side chair made comfortable by plump cushions – are definitely meant for sitting. They are positioned so that their occupants may overlook the results of Mr Gainey's newest enthusiasm: the design of *parterre* gardens, which for want of space elsewhere, he has miniaturised and grown in containers. A tiny form of euonymus and English boxwood, in both variegated and green form, makes patterns around standards of English holly and half-standard tree roses.

The outdoor living room is the place where house and garden merge, the very heart of the whole. Paths between the house, various sections of the garden, three glasshouses, and the driveway pass by small enclaves created using banks of potted plants where chairs, benches, and tables provide places to work and to rest.

The network of paths in this garden, rather

The third entrance gives access to a small garden in front of the house. Boxwoods edge a walk and a profusion of white flowers billow over the fence and onto small ovals of lawn.

The fourth entrance is the driveway on the right of the house where a cottage-style picket fence strains to contain what Mr Gainey calls his 'visitors' garden'. The fence appears to be losing the battle. Looking over the fence from the street, one catches a glimpse of a Cupid and a rustic bench nestled into the periphery of a great oval of lawn. The scene is dreamlike, coloured blue-green by an enormous white oak, *Quercus alba*. 'This tree,' states Ryan Gainey, 'keeps me

than a single *grande allée*, is one of its great delights. Because the ways are circuitous, they are an adventure to travel, rich in intrigue and surprise. Along the way are artfully composed 'vignettes' to be viewed at the side of the path or through small clearings. Urns, clusters of potted plants, shells, Beatrix Potter rabbits, chickens, kewpie dolls, flamingos, and other pieces of Mr Gainey's wonderful collection of American road-side art combine with plants to form tableaux.

'They're very simple,' he says of the artefacts he collects and uses in these vignettes, 'no matter how simple or how fine a thing is, it's all the same: it's the romance, the feeling that it evokes.'

Coming upon one of these pieces, isolated and emerging from a tangle of greenery, is a little like finding some remnant of a lost civilisation in the jungle. A great jug, veiled by irises or half-buried under Virginia creeper, suggests — if only for an instant — lost and ancient gardens in faraway places. Black-and-white-faced kewpie dolls, the traditional prizes for carnival games of chance, recall summer nights in little South Carolina towns with the scent of cotton candy and calliope music in the air. A shiny mirror globe, called a 'gazing ball', entwined with flamingos, was once the pride, in an age of American innocence, of a southern lawn.

There are monuments to the great gardens of England in hard-won delphinium spires and grids of vegetables and herbs; visions of Italian gardens in decorated water jugs and carefully shaped evergreens; and, in particular, love and nostalgia for the rural South where plaster chickens strutted on the front lawn and gazing balls once reflected the known world.

More than artefacts and plants, however, Ryan Gainey feels that 'people have influenced me more than any particular style — that is to say people who . . . create a garden that is wonderful because it is filled with the goodness of all that has become that person.'

IAN HAMILTON-FINLAY

VISUAL CONUNDRUMS

There's a clue as to what to expect in Ian Hamilton-Finlay's garden when you arrive at the gate to his property, set in the wall of a narrow lane near Dunsyre in Lanarkshire. A quotation from Heraclitus in immaculate Roman lettering greets you: 'The way up and the way down are one and the same'. Hamilton-Finlay clearly admires the style of Heraclitus's pre-Socratic brooding. With an enviable reputation as a concrete poet, and a great literary stylist himself, Hamilton-Finlay is here paying tribute to one of the earliest literary figures who recognised that the essence of nature is flourishing new growth followed by inevitable decay. There could be no more appropriate and stylish quotation at the entrance to a garden.

Ian Hamilton-Finlay believes that gardens should appeal to all the senses: not merely be lawns on which to play croquet. As well as inspiring calmness or animation, they ought, he believes, to be capable of provoking thought, both serious and trivial. And to accomplish this, he has revived the art of emblematic gardening which died out in Britain in the seventeenth century.

Emblematic gardens have existed for centuries. The Romans used to created them, as did the Italian Renaissance princes. These were gardens in which the arrangement of plants and inanimate objects could be viewed on two levels.

They could simply provide pleasure with their pleasing shapes, colours and compositions, but they could also provoke thought in that each element was intended as a symbol of something else. The Elizabethans planted triangular beds which appealed to the eye and, as a symbol of the Trinity, to the heart and mind as well. Similarly, shrubs and trees cut into ambitious topiary forms were often grouped in dozens to symbolise the twelve apostles.

Although the tradition of emblematic gardening died early in Europe, in China and Japan it still persists. There, every tiny element in even quite large gardens is symbolic of something else: raked gravel can represent rippled water or a beach; awkwardly zigzagging stepping stones preclude thoughtless progress and represent the rugged road through life; as it changes through the seasons, a single clearly exposed and exquisite plant serves as a reminder of the passage of time.

It was in this spirit that Ian Hamilton-Finlay began to transform the surrounds of a typical hill-farmstead into one of Britain's most provoking and rewarding gardens.

As visitors climb the rough three-quarter-mile track on to a flank of the Pentland Hills, they may recall the Heraclitus quotation with some apprehension. But when they reach the farmstead, the breadth of the view which confronts

Ian Hamilton-Finlay thinks that people are reluctant to read inscriptions in gardens unless they are part of artefacts such as sundials. So, as a poet with a lot to say, he has placed many sundials around his gardens – all of them thought-provoking and handsomely made

165

166

them quickly sweeps such mundane considerations aside. Even if some ignore their deeper implications, every gardener will rejoice in the beautiful and appropriately planted areas which Hamilton-Finlay has developed from the farm and its surrounding hills.

There wasn't much there when he arrived: a sparse scattering of rowans and scotch pine which hardly softened a very rugged and windy place. But now, with sheltering hedges and walls and dense tree and shrub planting, he has created many areas of calm. What was formerly the dungheap in the cattle yard has become an intriguing garden. Narrow, winding, partially paved paths disappear into thickly canopied small copses. There is a largish water feature and there are flowering plants growing abundantly within the shelter of the old farm buildings, one of which has been given a highly decorative façade to become a temple. Beyond the buildings, he has dammed a burn flowing from the upper slopes of the hill to make an impressive lake.

But these are achievements which could have been accomplished by any talented gardener with the time and enthusiasm. What makes Little Sparta (Hamilton-Finlay's name for the place) different is the richness and significance of its artefacts. And, for those who enjoy their nature well touched by the hand of man, they offer a remarkable and stylish contribution to the art of the garden.

Among hundreds of prompts to the imagination, Hamilton-Finlay has developed several clearly identifiable themes. Born on a bootlegger's cutter in the West Indies and living now in a country where no point is more than 60 miles distant from the sea, he is much preoccupied by what he calls 'maritime mythology'. The rolling hills of Lanarkshire which he overlooks remind him of ocean waves: the sigh of breezes through twigs and foliage recalls the cry of wind through rigging. To emphasise the connection, he has

worked with great contemporary craftsmen to create a host of maritime images. Cut into hundreds of stepping stones, there are profiles of just about every type of craft and the names of vessels which have worked from Scottish ports.

To beckon the eye over the waters of the lake, there is a marble model of a paper boat, symbolising the innocence of childhood adventure; beyond is the beautifully functional shape of a conning tower on an atomic submarine – reminiscent too of the sinister fin of a killer shark.

Instead of conventional bird-baths, there are miniature stone replicas of American and Russian aircraft carriers whose helicopter landing pads are perfectly scaled to serve as perches for drinking or bathing sparrows. Lurking among the dark shadows beneath the lower fronds of evergreen conifers, a stone replica of a Nautilus submarine produces a frisson of surprise.

Being a poet, Hamilton-Finlay understands the potency of the written word. 'But,' he says, 'people find it unacceptable in a natural setting unless it is inscribed upon a sundial or something resembling a memorial tablet.' So, in his garden, he has thirty-odd sundials and as many tablets –

all of them superbly crafted and inscribed with words soothing or provocative. There is much wit. For example: the elegiac inscription in the classical manner alongside a circular temple of young sycamore trees which simply says 'Bring Back the Birch'.

The cut-stone plinths stationed at the bottom of the trunks of a line of growing trees so that the trees appear to be growing out of them like columns are certainly very witty and stylish. Equally witty is the stepping stone inscribed with the form of iris leaves and set in the lawn at the feet of a growing iris. 'We get so little sun here to make shadows that we decided to make some of our own,' Hamilton-Finlay explained. A similar sense of fun inspired him to hang an inscribed stone tablet among the branches of a tree like a giant botanical label, and one cannot help but smile at the splendidly sculpted raised bed for two dandelion plants which makes a 'dandelion clock' among the many sundials.

167

Surrounded by a ring of sycamores, this beautifully carved stone tablet is designed to provoke thought as well as to provide a giggle

What nicer way to make a dandelion clock – and a comment about the passage of time? Each year new clumps are dug up from a meadow and replanted in holes in the stone which were expressly excavated to take them

Like most vegetable-growers, Ian Hamilton-Finlay has problems with birds, and his stylish solution has been to make a screen of real fishing net slung over poles.

Visual transpositions are another mode of expression which Hamilton-Finlay obviously enjoys. Two of the best examples are the re-creation of a romantic landscape by the French painter Claude Lorraine and the little turf island at the margin of the lake which echoes a drawing by Dürer, and is 'signed' by a small tablet with Dürer's signature.

When asked how he would advise on designing a garden, Ian Hamilton-Finlay suggested opening the back door and 'hurling a shrub out and then planting it where it lands. That's sure to create a problem and, in solving it and the next problem which is bound to be created by the solution, you will ultimately end up with a garden.' This approach, coupled with an ability to allow personal enthusiasms to be expressed in gardening terms, would produce a result which would 'embody the individual vision of the gardener and not just be a repetition of the tired ideas propagated by the gardening gurus.'

A re-creation of Dürer's famous drawing of 'The Great Piece of Turf' as an island at the edge of Ian Hamilton-Finlay's lake. Note the tablet inscribed with Dürer's initials

Beautiful as a sail but with inherent menace too, this sculpture of the conning tower of a nuclear submarine, which Ian Hamilton-Finlay calls 'Nuclear Sail', dominates one edge of the lake which he created by damming a burn

FUNDAMENTALISTS

*For the Douglas garden,
Steve Martino
concentrated the plant
elements to be found
naturally in the
surrounding desert*

JACK CHANDLER

WINE COUNTRY

Only an hour's drive from foggy San Francisco, landscape architect Jack Chandler's own garden is located in California's sunny Napa Valley. Describing it as 'in the heart of wine-growing country,' however, is an understatement. Not only does the house incorporate parts of an old vineyard house, it is surrounded by acres of working vineyard.

Wine-growers from Southern Europe, who emigrated to California, found in the Napa Valley a familiar landscape and a superb climate for viticulture. Today, with vineyards stretching toward low hills on the horizon, sunny skies, and heat-tolerant vegetation, the area is still reminiscent of the Mediterranean. Jack Chandler has played upon this similarity, consciously incorporating classical elements into his garden.

Inspired by visions of Italian gardens, Mr Chandler added 'water, citrus trees,' and 'muted colours.' A crowning touch, an old, grandly spreading olive tree that stands between two sections of the garden, was already there when he bought the property. In position and spirit, the olive tree is the centre of this garden. Yet the parts that radiate around it do not conform to the expected, symmetrical plan. Instead, they are asymmetrical, apportioned according to use. Thus, classical components – colour, water, vegetation – are put together in a thoroughly contemporary way.

Depending upon the time of day, the olive shades one of two separate and unequal gardens. One is a secluded, secret garden that is walled for maximum privacy; it is a place for reading, working outside, or quiet reflection. The other is an area designed for activity and entertainment that is open to the vista of vineyards and low hills. It is in this open, outdoor entertaining and living area that Old World elements merge with contemporary California style. The black-bottomed pool with waterspouts to fill the air with the cooling sounds of water is not just for looking and thinking cool thoughts, but for swimming. Likewise, a second small pool is a whirlpool spa. Adjacent to both pool and whirlpool, a flagstone terrace is softened here and there by seemingly random clumps of fountain grass, *Pennisetum*, that bloom pink and rustle in the slightest breeze. These are plants as delightful to look upon as they are easy to maintain.

At one end of the terrace, shading a seating and dining area, is a pergola constructed of lodgepole pine. It is a lovely place to sit and contemplate the low hills in the distance or the acres of vineyards that surround the garden. As the sun sinks, the pool's silver surface reflects the fading brilliance of the sky.

Dividing the pool and surrounding terrace from a stretch of lawn behind the house is a mixed planting of the low-growing, often

*Clumps of pink-seeded
fountain grass soften the
paving and terrace
around Jack Chandler's
pool*

*The simple pole-work of
this poolside pergola
casts intriguing shadows
while supporting
climbers which offer
welcome shade as they
develop during the
warmer months*

Reminiscent of an Italian garden in containers, a cluster of potted plants surrounds an olive tree in a secluded section of Jack Chandler's garden

glaucous plants one associates with the Mediterranean. Among these are lavenders, salvias, santolinas, and Russian sage. The muted colours and low, spreading forms are repeated throughout the garden. The pool and private gardens around the olive flank one side of the house. On the other, next to a driveway that leads from the street to a barn, is a deep border given over to a lovely and fragrant mixture of perennials and herbs that spills over onto the concrete, softening hard edges. Perovskia blooms violet and the

silvery greys of santolina, lavender and artemesia dazzle in the morning light. Yet Mr Chandler has planted not only for form and colour, but for fragrance. In spring the sweet scents of lemon and orange blossoms fill the air. Later, others – sweet olive (*Osmanthus fragrans*), star jasmine (*Jasminum polyanthum*), and honeysuckle – come in fragrant and welcome succession.

While soft forms and colours soothe the eyes and sweet scents delight the nose, the placement

of interesting objects intrigues. There are Italianate terracotta pots, and bundles of grape stakes carefully placed around the pool and terrace. The pots, filled with bouquets of dried grasses, rest on shelves built into the side of the pool and the whirlpool.

Between the house and a perennial-bordered lawn, a long path leads under the verandah from driveway to pool terrace. Both ends have been provided with foci. In the shade of the olive on the pool terrace side is a stone carving of a Mayan-looking sun; at the other end another very fitting subject serves as focus – the intricate and rusty forms of a wine press.

Like the inclusion of this sculpture, the delights of Jack Chandler's garden, both visual and olfactory, are pleasant, understated, and – if unexpected – utterly fitting. With an Italian inspiration and a modern, functional plan, it is a place of quiet contentment that adorns but doesn't compete with the subtle, sunny landscape of California's wine country.

Deep verandahs and shady trees are a vital feature of any garden in a Mediterranean climate

WILLIAM H. FREDERICK JR

OVER-SIMPLIFICATION

William H. Frederick Jr must rank as one of the most interesting landscape architects currently working in the north-eastern United States.

He is very cautious about the use of the word 'style'. 'I must confess that I am turned off by it as it infers stylish, which infers fashionable . . . If by "style" you mean a work of art with flair, then I am comfortable.' He says that he particularly enjoys 'good contemporary design which empha-sises simplified (even if sophisticated) form and carefully controlled exuberance of colour and texture.'

In their own garden Mr and Mrs Frederick have adopted this seemingly sober approach with spectacular results. Three notable features there proclaim him a true master of garden design.

The Fredericks' garden is on a dry south-facing hillside and at the bottom of a shallow valley cut by a brook which in high summer

Moss and liverworts carpet an earth sculpture made from battered clay in the pool of Mr and Mrs William Frederick Jr's Stream Valley Garden. Since the clay always remains moist, the mosses and liverworts thrive

176

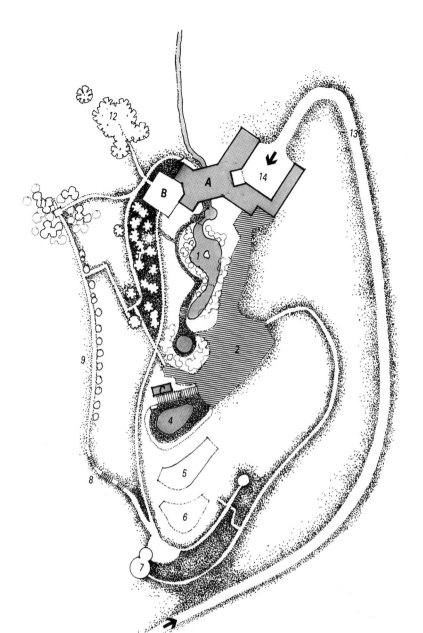

A House bridge across stream
B Studio garden: colour experimentation:
espaliers, topiary & herbs
C 1850 spring house: swimming pool,
modern grape arbour for shade

1 Stream valley garden: moss island,
waterfalls and azaleas
2 Game lawn
3 Grape arbour
4 Swimming pool
5 Vegetables: four-square system
6 Nursery test area
7 Winter garden: stone paved sun pocket
8 Hillside meadow: railway sleeper steps,
set on contour
9 Dark green, grey and white shrub path:
for summer evenings
10 Tree wistarias
11 Calocedrus: orange, chartreuse and
lavender
12 Persimmon grove
13 Approach road
14 Entrance court

177

would run nearly dry. By building stone walls to canalise its course in places, and a series of weirs, Frederick has ensured that it holds a decent depth of water all year round, thus creating long uninterrupted reaches, extended vistas and a large, attractive pond.

Overshadowed by elegant mature ash trees, the moist shore of the pond is thickly clad with moss to form a surrounding 'moss lawn', so that the black, almost circular mirror of water is held within a dark-green bowl. Weed growth is minimised, leaving most of the water surface clear to reflect what Frederick calls an 'earth sculpture' — a mound of smoothly battered clay which emerges as an island from the water and which, because it is habitually damp, has become encrusted with a mixture of greenish-brown moss and liverwort. This unusual water garden feature was designed for the Fredericks by Conrad Hamerman, formerly a student of one of William

Frederick's idols, the great Brazilian Roberto Burle Marx (see Introduction). Apart from capitalising on the nature of the site, Frederick feels that the moss island is 'a distillation of the essence of the stream valley site, in the same terms that many Japanese gardens are distillations of classical Japanese scenery.'

The exuberant 'tree' wistaria garden is one of Frederick's own inventions, developed from a technique pioneered by an aunt of his who trained wistaria vines into small trees by attaching them to frames. The system worked so well on the dry lower slopes of the valley that Frederick decided to give the whole area over to it. The two giant steel-girder frames supporting

the wistaria have a very strong sculptural interest and impact. He has painted them matt brown, employing what he calls 'focused over-emphasis'. 'Just for the hell of it, one of them resembles the structure of a round-top shade tree and the other a conifer – a folly if you will.'

Frederick then decided to allow much of the natural vegetation on the upper slopes of the garden to remain undisturbed while, exercising minimal management, a flower meadow was encouraged to prosper at the feet of the trees and shrubs. Some sort of stepped path was necessary to gain access to and enjoy this steep area, particularly after heavy rain. Frederick's solution shows how even mundane features can be ac-

One of the impressive sculptural frames which William Frederick Jr uses to support climbing wistaria

178

complished with great panache. As is usual in non-formal gardens, heavy timber beams hold back the earth base of steps cut into the hillside. However, both the width and depth of individual steps varies greatly, though their height is a uniform and comfortable 9 inches. The width of a particular step was mostly determined by aesthetic considerations and, since no attempt was made to even the slope, steps were created only when necessary to mount the contours. On the shallower areas of the slope fewer risers were necessary and the tread surfaces became extended to form mini-plateaux.

In practice, this means that, when observed from the house, the eye is led up the hillside by an obvious crosshatching of timbers following as closely as possible the line which Frederick felt would be most pleasing. The result is a sort of rustic *scala regia* leading to an area which has all the attributes of a natural shrine. It's an area where an observer feels that nature at its most beautiful has been allowed to dominate.

Frederick advises gardeners to 'study the site and decide how best you can capture its essence by over-simplification; examine the interests and activities that will be the expression of your personality in the garden and settle upon a dramatisation of one particularly personal aspect – perhaps as I did by creating a folly.'

Contoured steps mount the hillside meadow in the William Frederick Jr garden

STEVE MARTINO

ARIZONA XERISCAPE

Even in the face of overwhelming reasons to abandon them, some customs die hard. In the arid states of the American Southwest, settlers long ago brought firmly fixed ideas of what landscapes and gardens should look like – generally the remembered images of New England's green hills, or those, greener still, of England, Ireland, or Northern Europe. Then they proceeded to replace the existing climate-appropriate vegetation with exotics from other climatic zones and do whatever else was necessary to turn memory into reality. Extensive irrigation systems to support lawn and flower gardens became commonplace in the Southwest and nobody questioned their use until very recently.

Now, however, with escalating water costs and water shortages and a new appreciation of native flora, southwestern gardens are undergoing a transformation. In the vanguard of those who seek to preserve the desert's singular beauty is Arizona native Steve Martino whose landscape architectural firm, Steve Martino & Associates, respects the desert environment and does so with great style.

Martino's design for the site development of the Mesa, Arizona residence of Cliff and Marilyn Douglas was hailed as a 'landmark example of appropriateness for a single-family dwelling in a desert environment,' by the Valley Forward Association who awarded the design a 'Crescordia' for environmental excellence. It isn't the first award he has received, nor is it likely to be the last.

'A big part of their criteria was thoughtful use of resources,' he explains. From the beginning, Steve Martino's purpose was 'to create a living environment compatible with natural desert surroundings as well as creating an aesthetic that is unmistakably desert derived.'

Borrowing colours, plants, materials, and forms from the desert environment, Steve Martino fashioned a garden oasis in perfect harmony with its surroundings. Now that the trees have grown up, the garden is a cool, stylish, and wonderfully luxurious theatre for the drama and majesty of the desert around it. Mimicking its surroundings, this garden condenses the random, widely spaced desert vegetation into densely planted, opulent ground cover. It is a dynamic garden, responding constantly to the strong, changing light of the desert sun.

Like the desert, the garden is dramatically transformed in the course of each day. Rosy magenta flowers of *Penstemon parryi*, and the pale lavender of masses of *Verbena gooddingii* sparkle in the strong, clean morning light. For an hour or two, foliage appears spring green again. As the sun rises, intense sunlight flattens forms and bleeds colours into monochrome. By midday

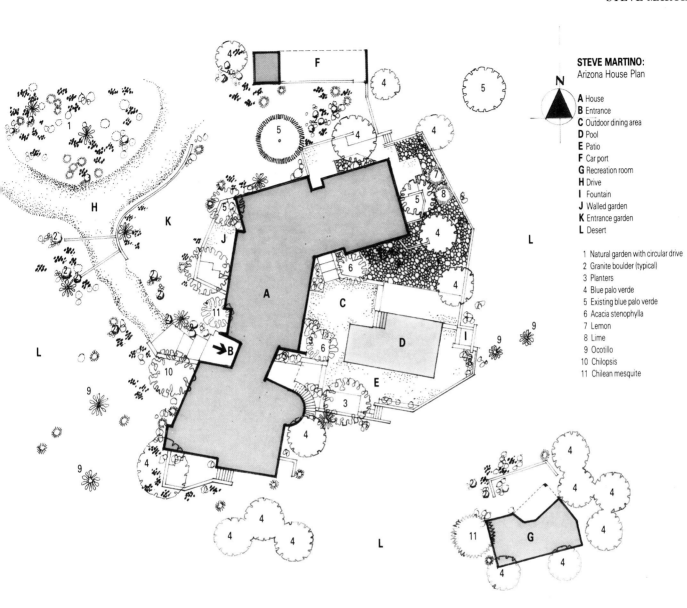

STEVE MARTINO:
Arizona House Plan

A House
B Entrance
C Outdoor dining area
D Pool
E Patio
F Car port
G Recreation room
H Drive
I Fountain
J Walled garden
K Entrance garden
L Desert

1 Natural garden with circular drive
2 Granite boulder (typical)
3 Planters
4 Blue palo verde
5 Existing blue palo verde
6 Acacia stenophylla
7 Lemon
8 Lime
9 Ocotillo
10 Chilopsis
11 Chilean mesquite

181

only the strongest, most distinct shapes – the ocotillos, the saguaro cacti and aloes – remain distinct. By late afternoon, the light softens and colour returns. House and garden glow rosy pink and the greens of acacias and ocotillos deepen to olive drab.

The path of the sun is a primary consideration when planning a house and garden in the desert. The harmonious relationship that was ultimately achieved between the Douglas house, garden and site required thoughtful placement of all the elements in relation to the sun and the contours of the land. The owners appreciate the desert and its unique plant and animal life and wished to disturb the pristine five-acre site as little as possible.

Both the entrance of the house, which is recessed to give protection from the sun, and the driveway face the west where an entrance garden welcomes visitors. The entrance door is located in the narrow waist of the hourglass-shaped house. From the front door one can look right through the house to a private garden and outdoor living area on the southeastern side and beyond to the great expanse of the desert.

Working closely with architect John Douglas, son of the owners, Steve Martino designed a complex of exterior walls, walks, patios, pool, retaining walls, and green-tiled fountain which follow the natural descent of the hillside through a series of levels. Although Martino describes the outdoor living area as 'tightly defined space', it is truly spacious. Because 'no desert [has been] given away to traditional lawn or yards,' a handsome allotment of space was allowed for this combination garden and outdoor living room. The garden room occupies three generous levels on the southeastern side of the house which correspond to the levels within the house. Six doors make it accessible to every part of the house. Most of the garden room is paved with Mexican tiles. Plants are grouped in planters and in unpaved space along the edges.

A three-foot-high masonry wall with a plaster finish to match the stucco of the house runs around the inside edge of this outdoor room, cleanly separating the virtually untouched desert landscape from the ordered, organised space and the decorative plants growing within the walls. As well as providing definition, the walls create a sense of shelter without blocking splendid vistas of the distant mountains and the surrounding desert. Steve Martino also favours low walls for the informal seating space that they offer. Because they are low, the walls suggest enclosure while keeping the garden utterly open to its surroundings. This sheltered openness and the fact that many of the same plants which occur naturally on the site are heavily concentrated around the patio make it an ideal meeting ground for the house and the surrounding countryside. There is a graceful transition between the man-made and the natural.

The foliage colours of the plants along the patio – aloe, salvia – are primarily the same dusty grey-greens of the native vegetation with mauves to echo the purple of the distant hills. Now and then a vibrant splash of colour from plants such as Bougainvillea 'Barbara Karst' enlivens the planting. The pale stucco of the house and walls, and the rosy clay-coloured Mexican tiles are earth tones, perfectly suited to the setting. While the colours of the patio clearly define the space, they do not jar but rather blend into the warm earth tones of the desert palette.

In the centre of the patio is a straight-sided pool of which one side also functions as the retaining wall for an elevated portion of patio. Lounge chairs on this level command a sweeping view of the desert. One can step down from here in two directions: towards the house, steps lead to the main patio floor which is continuous with the floor of the living room. Here a cosy outdoor dining area is just steps from the inside, shaded by an acacia, and sheltered by planters dense with salvia, penstemon, aloe, and agaves. On the desert side, steps lead to a cooling fountain and a small seating area set off by saguaro cacti and ocotillos.

Both fountain and pool bring visual and psychic relief to the dry desert setting. In colour, surface texture, sound, and form, water is an utterly foreign but welcome element here. A few inches below the main patio floor, the sheet of sparkling cool water provides interesting contrast in the garden as well as a fourth level of interest on the patio.

Along the house and walls are planting beds. These have been provided with small, manually operated, drip irrigation systems as the most economical means of supplying water when it is needed. The system can be controlled to drip one half gallon of water per hour that 'keeps wicking down into the ground.' Irrigation is confined to three areas close to the house and guest house. In these beds the plants have responded to the supplementary water with vigorous, lush growth. Elsewhere on the property, desert vegetation

Shadows of arid-climate natives play against the blank walls of the Douglas house. They were conceived as part of the initial design of the garden door

survives without any human intervention.

'The use of native and desert plant material,' states Steve Martino, 'is essential. If architecture [or] landscape architecture is to be of any significance here as an art form, it must respond to the desert environment.'

Within the garden and in the planted areas close to the house, communities of desert natives are highly concentrated for dense ground cover. In addition, drought-tolerant, sun-loving ornamentals have been added for colour and interest. Ocotillo, *Fouquieria splendens*, an odd spidery-looking southwestern native plant absorbs water through its woody trunk. After rain the stems

suddenly grow leaves. The century plant, *Agave americana*, prickly pears and Indian figs, *Opuntia*, are similarly sculptural plants with great presence. They retain their own identity even when the brightest sunlight drains colour and form from less distinct individuals.

'Spiked agave and prickly pears cast wonderful shadows. I like and use shadow a lot – at night, too, when I put spotlights on agaves,' says Martino. Shadows, playing against stark house walls and across the tile paving, change hourly, adding depth and interest to the plantings. In the bright desert light, colour can be intense without ever appearing harsh. Bougainvillea, *Aloe*

The structure and landscape design of this Arizona residence are perfectly suited to the desert environment. Dominating the front garden of existing saguaros, opuntias and brittle bush is a wiry ocotillo

184

saponaria, with its orange flowers, yellow-flowered creosote (*Larrea*), Verbena, Butterfly weed (*Asclepias*), Arizona yellow bells, Texas red salvia (*S. Greggii*), Mexican red bird (*Pedilanthus tithymaloides*), and 'San Diego Red' hibiscus add welcome spots of colour.

At the entrance to the house are two gardens. The more public one occupies both sides of a wide gravel entrance walk that leads to a set of steps with very large treads and low risers. To the right of the steps, a low wall is softened by mounds of penstemon, brittle bush, and salvia. Behind and among these is a desert willow, a humming bird bush and prickly pear cacti.

On the left side of the steps is a naturalistically planted semicircle. It is dominated by two wiry ocotillos and underplanted with brittle bush. Small, existing saguaros, creosote, and prickly pear cacti cast shadows against a stark white wall that encloses a private garden accessible only from inside the house. Chilean mesquite and and acacia cast shade that is shared by both gardens.

When the house was first built, windows on the western side were unprotected from the setting sun. 'The west was a real problem,' says Steve Martino. 'The windows had no sun protection, but there was a beautiful view down into the valley.' Because the owners treasured that view, they didn't want to eliminate or diminish the size of the windows. Instead, Martino added trees which eventually grew to shade the windows and the private patio. 'Now you go out on the patio and you're really under a cover. The trees have grown up and you look through them to see the valley.'

Beyond the house walls, the desert remains untouched, or in places where it was disturbed in the building process, it has been re-vegetated with native plants. An island in the circular driveway in front of the house combines an untouched, existing stand of native vegetation, in-

cluding saguaros, with a naturalistic planting of Mexican red bird, agaves, prickly pears, Indian figs, and ocotillos transplanted from other places on the site.

'A simple native plant palette was the theme' of this garden in the desert, explains Steve Martino, adding, 'the excitement comes from the contrast of the ordered and refined elements that reflect man set against the fantastic wild natural landscape.'

In the Douglas garden, plants of the desert have been placed in a setting that suits them both aesthetically and environmentally. In return, desert plants tie the house and garden to their natural surroundings.

'Rather than deny the desert or make apologies for it,' states Steve Martino, 'we have embraced it.'

Shadow patterns play a part in the design of this garden. Here a railing casts shadow against a stucco wall. Later the Mexican fence-post cactus, here planted with purple trailing lantana, will cast another shadow. The wall is embellished with one of Mrs Douglas's handmade tiles – each of which celebrates a desert bird or animal

185

STUART PITTENDRIGH

POOLSIDE DOWN-UNDER

Poolside socialising is one of the more memorable delights of Australian life. And it is probable that, when all other recollections have faded for exiles in chillier lands, it remains the most persistent image. Wine and grilled meat to accompany chatter both trivial and profound under a leafy canopy are to many quintessential to civilised life. That is obviously a consideration which figures high in Stuart Pittendrigh's list of priorities and that of many of the clients for whom he designs gardens. It is certainly evident in the design of his own charming garden at Carlingford on the north shore of Sydney harbour.

There, unlike many landscapers designing gardens for a Mediterranean climate, he took into account the fact that, no matter how inviting a sparkling pool might be in the early morning or in the evening, too clear a view of its surface reflections at noon can be a head-splitting experience. To avoid that seemingly obvious but frequent error he has arranged a broken screen of vegetation to separate diners beneath his shady pergola from a too overt view of the pool's dazzling surface. Anyone seeking the reassurance of its soothing presence and potential for cooling hot blood can direct a glance through a hedge of foliage. But even diners facing towards the pool can dine without discomfort. And they will certainly enjoy the style and originality of the setting.

A light touch and impeccable taste typify all of Pittendrigh's work, which he stamps with his own personality by the subtlest of means. A good example is the way in which much of the poolside dining area is overhung by pergola timbers which are cantilevered from the main roof frame. Here he has gently modified a conventional structure to give it a style of his own. He has also lightened the appearance of the vertical columns by adopting the North American technique of making them into composite structures. Instead of a single over-robust timber they are composed of two much lighter members bolted together and separated by thin wooden spacers or the horizontal roof elements which they clasp. This method of construction is very strong but it is light in appearance since objects can be seen through the gaps between the elements.

While elsewhere in the garden the planting is permanent, in the barbecue and dining area Pittendrigh has built flexibility into his design by arranging to have most of the plants in pots and tubs. This means that, as in a theatre set, they can be moved about to change the scene or even be completely removed to a safer place elsewhere in the garden if large scale entertaining is planned.

He has selected the plants which he uses in this way very carefully to ensure that they offer the

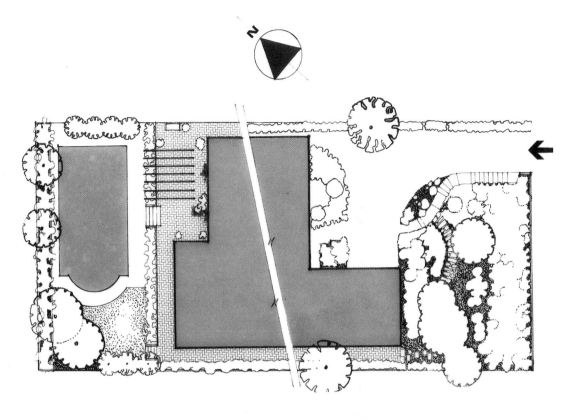

A House
B Brick paved terrace
C Pergola
D Barbecue
E Swimming pool
F Lawn
G Brick pathway

 1 Dicksonia antartica
 2 Trachelospermum jasminoides
 3 Thymus
 4 Cotoneaster horizontalis
 5 Iris
 6 Ajuga reptans
 7 Rhododendrons
 8 Agapanthus
 9 Sabina vulgaris
10 Murraya paniculata
11 Russelia equisetiformis
12 Bauera rubioides
13 Sapium sebiferum
14 Eucalyptus
15 Gordonia axillaris
16 Plumbago capensis
17 Nandina domestica
18 Viola hederacea
19 Cistus
20 Acer palmatum
21 Juniperus conferta
22 Sabina vulgaris
23 Grevillea X 'Robyn Gordon'
24 Betula pendula
25 Camellia sasangua
26 Bamboo
27 Celsima
28 Gardenia augusta
29 Banksia leptospermum
30 Erigeron

187

*By making a feature of
such commonplace
subjects as the charming
little Western Australian
daisy, designers like
Stuart Pittendrigh are
doing much to revive an
interest in native flora*

The cantilevered pergola in Stuart Pittendrigh's garden overhangs many plants established in tubs. This enables them to be moved into more prominent positions when they are offering their most impressive display or to be removed altogether if more room is needed for large parties

188

maximum of effect while occupying the minimum of ground area. A good example is his use of the black-stemmed bamboo *Phyllostachys nigra* which, from a smallish tub, can raise a dense head of elegant foliage to a height of eight to ten feet. Among less spectacular plants, Agapanthus 'Headbourne Hybrid' and the frothy evergreen fern *Nephrolepis exalta* have strong individual characteristics which make them outstanding when grown in pots.

To compensate for the lack of ground planting in the dining area, Pittendrigh has placed heavy emphasis on the use of hanging baskets planted with dense evergreen ferns to reinforce the over-head canopy. To prevent them from seeming too dominant and forbidding he has ensured that the pergola roof structure is suspended well above the heads of even the tallest standing visitors.

Gardenias, dicksonias and camellias feature among the permanent planting beyond the pool and contribute to the exotic appeal of its setting.

On the other side of the house hewn-rock walls and a scattering of large boulders make a fine background for a host of native Australian plants mixed with a few beautiful imports from other warm places. Here russelias, gordonias and banksias mix their charms with the perfume of *Trachelospermum jasminoides* and the haunting fragrance of sun-cooked eucalyptus. There has also been much use of evergreen ground covers and a heavy mulching with ground tree-bark to suppress weeds.

Like all good designers, Stuart Pittendrigh always seems to find ways of setting plants to maximise their impact. By such tricks as isolating a thick clump of the very commonplace Western Australian daisy *Brachycome ibiridifolia* at the head of a flight of steps he has emphasised its charm and bestowed upon it the dignity of some-thing much more costly and exotic. It is in such small and telling touches that one detects the hand of a real master.

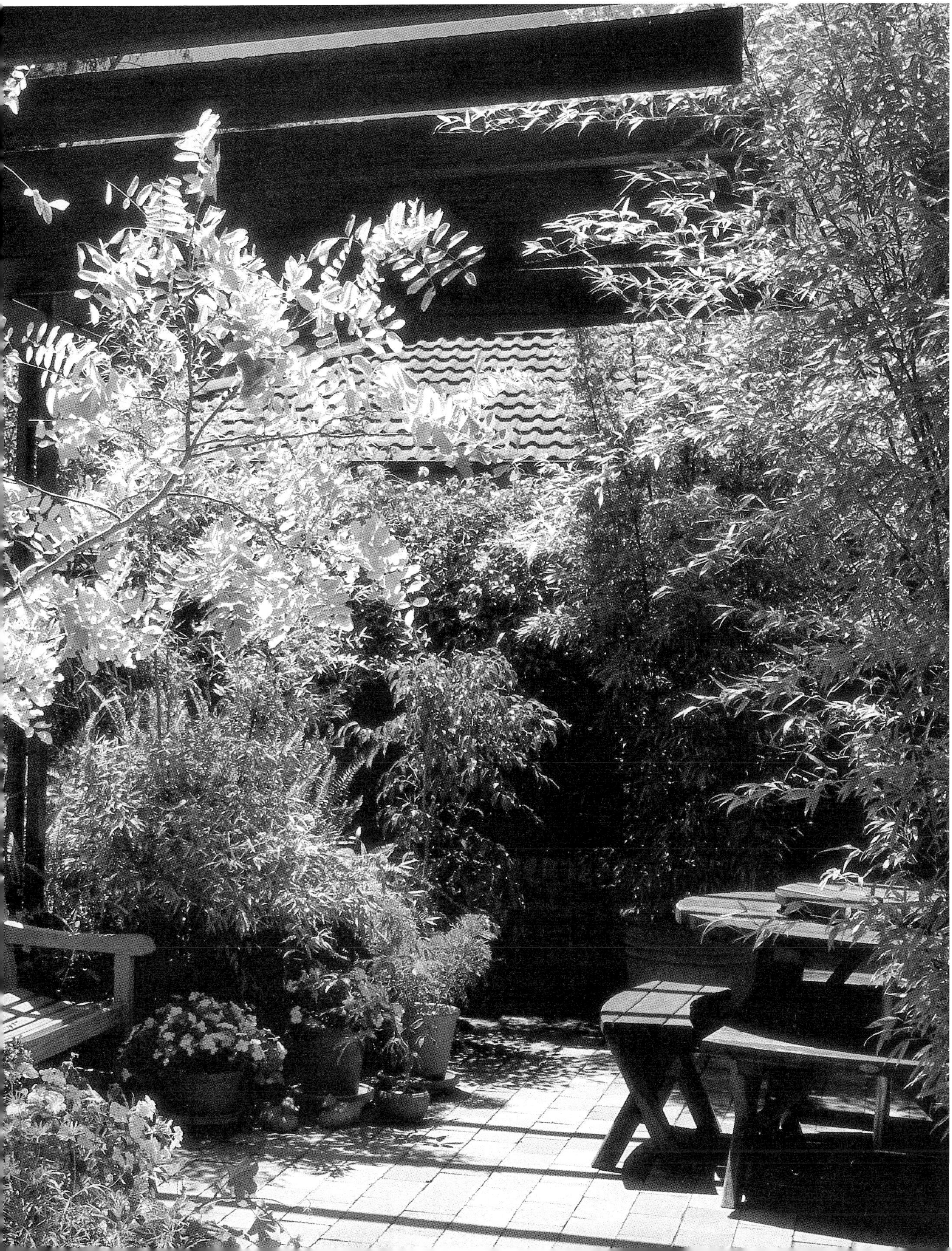

PLANTS WITH STYLE

Given the right situation in the garden, there are few plants which have not got something attractive to offer. And even the least significant or most commonplace shouldn't necessarily be disregarded on the grounds of either their scale or the fact that they are seen growing just about everywhere. Tiny mosses, for example, can look breathtaking when established as a thick velvety carpet surrounding a woodland pool. While they are perhaps too frequent denizens of surburban gardens to warrant much attention as individual plants, simple nasturtiums or pot marigolds can look splendid when grown as great sheets beneath white barked birch or groves of olives.

In view of what has been said above, it might seem invidious to single out for special mention plants which seem to be endowed with that quality which we recognise as style. However, there is little doubt that some plants have much more obvious and striking characteristics than others which, when given a prominent position, do much to impart a very particular character to the area surrounding them. From among the vast range of plants available to the modern garden designer we have prepared the following list of those which we consider to be outstanding. Not all of them will be available as young plants at garden centres. But it would always be worthwhile trying to find them at specialist nurseries or growing them from seed.

190

Annuals and biennials which will tolerate some shade

Briza maxima
Digitalis lanata
Lupinus argenteus
Nicotiana alata 'Lime Green'

Annuals and biennials for a sunny situation

Althaea rosea nigra
Lavatera trimestris 'Loveliness'
Senecio maritima 'Silver Dust'

Herbaceous perennials which will tolerate some shade

Acanthus longifolus
Aconitum fischeri
Anemone japonica 'Kriemhilde'
Anemone narcissiflora
Aquilegia caerulea
Asplenum scolopendrium 'Undulatum'
Astilbe 'Ostrich Plume'
Astrantia major alba
Anthurium felix-femina
Avena candida
Cimicifuga racemosa
Cortaderia selloana
Dicentra spectabilis
Epimedium grandiflorum
Euphorbia robbiae
Festuca ovina glauca
Helleborus corsicus
Hemerocallis 'Lark Song'
Hosta sieboldiana elegans
Lamium maculatum 'Chequers'
Lychnis viscaria 'Splendens Plena'
Malva moschata alba
Miscanthus sinensis 'Silver Fern'
Pachysandra terminalis
Paeonia lactiflora
Papaver orientale 'May Queen'
Primula auricula
Primula denticulata alba
Stachys lanata
Thalictrum dipterocarpum
Tiarella wherryi

Herbaceous perennials which enjoy full sun

Achillea 'Cerise Queen'
Agapanthus patens
Artemesia absinthum
Artemesia stelleriana
Centaurea montana
Clematis integrifolia
Cyanara cardunculus
Delphinium elatum 'Black Knight'
Echinops ritro
Eryngium bourgatti
Euphorbia wulfenii
Geranium 'Playboy Speckles'
Geranium wallichianum 'Buxton's Blue'
Gypsophila paniculata
Gypsophila paniculata 'Pink Star'
Kniphofia erecta
Iris foetidissima
Iris pallida variegata
Oenothera missouriensis
Physalis franchetii
Pyrethrum ptarmicaeflorum 'Silver Feather'
Scabiosa graminifolia
Sidalcea 'Loveliness'
Verbascum olympicum
Verbascum virginica alba

Water and waterside plants which will tolerate some shade

Gunnera manicata
Iris laevigata
Lysichitum americanus
Nymphea 'James Brydon'
Nymphea laydekeri purpurata
Rheum palmatum rubrum

Water and waterside plants which enjoy full sun

Acorus columnus variegatus
Pontederia cordata
Zantedeschia aethiopica 'Crowborough'

Climbers and wall plants which will tolerate some shade

Clematis 'Duchess of Edinburgh'
Clematis 'John Warren'
Clematis orientalis
Cytisus battandieri
Hedera 'Goldheart'
Hydrangea petiolaris
Hydrangea sargentiana
Lonicera japonica aureoreticulata
Lonicera periclymenum 'Serotina'
Trachelospermum jasminoides
Vitis coignetiae
Vitis vinifera 'Brandt'

Climbers and wall plants which enjoy full sun

Actinidia kolomikta
Fremontodendron californicum 'Californian Glory'
Lathyrus nervosus

Shrubs which will tolerate some shade

Aralia elata
Arundinaria nitida
Camellia japonica 'Marguerite Gouillon'
Buddleia globosa
Carpentaria californica
Corylus avellana contorta
Fatsia japonica
Garrya elliptica
Hydrangea macrophylla 'Blue Wave'
Mahonia 'Charity'
Pieris 'Forest Flame'
Rhododendron cinnabarinum
Rhus typhina lacinata
Salix caprea pendula
Symphoricarpus doorenbosii 'Magic Berry'
Viburnum tinus
Yucca filamentosa

Shrubs which enjoy full sun

Artemesia arborescens
Buxus sempervirens pendula
Convolvulus cneorum
Datura sanguinea
Helichrysum lanatum
Paeonia suffruticosa
Petovskia atriplicifolia 'Blue Spire'
Phormium tenax
Salvia officinalis
Spirea cantoniensis lanceata
Yucca flaccida 'Ivory'

Trees which will tolerate some shade

Acer griseum
Acer pennsylvanicum
Arbutus unedo
Betula jacquemontii
Cedrus atlantica glauca pendula
Corylus maxima purpurea
Juniperus communis 'Hibernica'
Magnolia grandiflora 'Exmouth'
Malus 'Golden Hornet'
Picea breweriana
Pyrus salicifolia pendula
Quercus ilex
Sambucus racemosa plumosa aurea
Sophora japonica pendula

Trees which enjoy full sun

Catalpha bignonioides
Cornus florida
Davidia involucrata
Ficus carica
Paulownia tomentosa

Bulbs, corms and tubers which tolerate some shade

Cardiocrinum giganteum
Fritillaria meleagris
Iris reticulata
Lilium auratum 'Lavender Princess'
Lilium regale
Narcissus poeticus recurvus
Tulipa praestans 'Fusilier'

Bulbs, corms and tubers which enjoy full sun

Allium cernum
Crinum moorei
Eremurus × shelford
Gladiolus carneus
Nerine 'Bowdenii Pink'

Roses which will tolerate some shade while enjoying full sun

191

Rosa 'Mary Rose'
Rosa mundi
Rosa rubrifolia
Rosa 'Camieux'
Rosa 'Graham Thomas'
Rosa 'Grouse'
Rosa 'Madame Alfred Carrière'
Rosa moyesii 'Geranium'
Rosa 'Reine des violettes'
Rosa spinosissima

ACKNOWLEDGEMENTS

The authors would like to thank all those people who so generously gave of their time to discuss this book or make suggestions about its contents. In particular, we are greatly indebted to those people who garden with style for allowing us access to their gardens and providing invaluable information about them. Wilfred Chambers deserves special thanks for the admirable way in which he interpreted what were often little more than scribbles and made them into notable illustrations.

Rosemary Verey, Michael Balchin, Carole Rosenberg, Arabella Lennox Boyd, William Frederick Jr, Sir Roy Strong, The Countess of Rosse, Steve Martino, A. E. Bye, Jack Jefferies, Julian Shuckburgh, Kathy Van Gorder and David Hicks all provided invaluable help. We must also thank Jonathan Weaver, Jeremy Cockayne and all the photographers for their unsparing efforts on our behalf.

Lastly, we are grateful to David Reynolds and Jane Carr for their courage in publishing and care in editing the manuscript.

192

Picture Credits

The authors are grateful to the following for permission to reproduce photographs: Sue Barnes 2, 88, 90; Mr and Mrs C. Graham Berwind Jr 141 top and bottom, 142 left and right, 143, 144 top, centre and bottom, 145; Clive Boursnell 139; Michael Boys Syndication 35, 39; John Brookes 80, 83, 84, 85, 86; Karl-Dietrich Buhler 27, 28, 32; Gilles Clement 1, 67 top and bottom, 69; George Clive 18, 20, 21; Jeremy Cockayne 16, 40, 42, 43, 44, 45, 155, 156; Arnaud Descat 15, 70; Alban Donohoe 47, 51, 53; Patrick Eyres 10, 14, 165, 168, 169; William H. Frederick Jr 176, 178, 179; The Garden Picture Library/Ron Sutherland 23, 25, 187, 189; *Good Housekeeping*/Marianne Majerus 153; Joe Holly 78, 79; Angelo Hornak 150; Alun T. Jones 123; Peter King 13; John Last 7, 98, 100; Arabella Lennox-Boyd 49 right; Carole Ottesen 55, 56, 57, 58, 61, 62, 65, 74, 75, 77, 112, 114, 115, 130, 131, 133, 162, 163, 170, 173 top and bottom, 174, 175, 183, 184, 185; Karin Ottesen 117; Hugh Palmer 105, 107, 108, 109; Dave Paterson 166, 167 top and bottom; Philippe Perdereau 8; Jill Posener 110, 121; Su Rogers 11, 12; Graham Rose 48, 97, 99, 103; Shirley Schmitke 9; Ben Taylor 157; J. W. Thomas 125; Jonathan Weaver 135, 136, 147, 149, 159; Malcolm Younger 91, 93, 94, 95.